Travels with George in Search of Ben Hur

and Other Meanderings

Travels with George in Search of Ben Hur

and Other Meanderings

Paul Ruffin

The University of South Carolina Press

Published by the University of South Carolina Press
Columbia, South Carolina 29208

www.sc.edu/uscpress

Manufactured in the United States of America

20 19 18 17 16 15 14 13 12 11 10 9 8 7 6 5 4 3 2 1

LIBRARY OF CONGRESS CATALOGING-IN-PUBLICATION DATA

Ruffin, Paul.
Travels with George in search of Ben Hur and other meanderings / Paul Ruffin.
p. cm.
ISBN 978-1-57003-986-7 (cloth : alk. paper)
I. Title.
PS3568.U362T73 2011
814'.54—DC22 2011001618

This book was printed on Glatfelter Natures, a recycled paper with 30 percent postconsumer waste content.

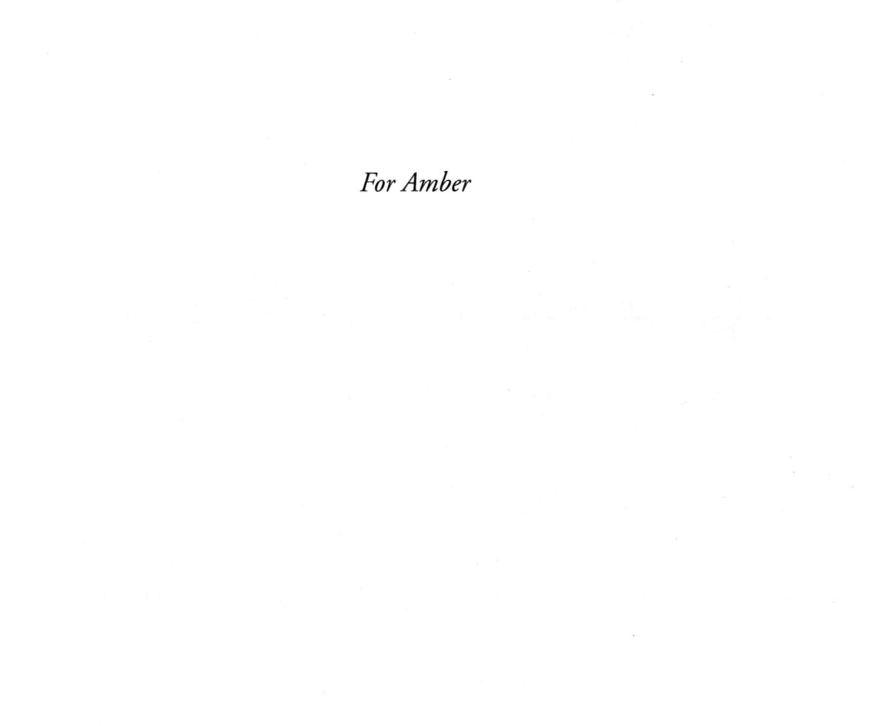

For Amber

Contents

Preface

Early on in my writing career I focused on little more than poetry—my first serious efforts and my initial publications were in that genre. It was only after I started a cattle operation outside Huntsville and for some reason began writing dramatic poems about cows and rabbits and drought and women (an odd stew there) that I realized how little more needed to be done to flesh them out into essays and stories.

This is not to say that I had not already written a whole lot of fiction and nonfiction. Whereas it is true that my love of poetry came from years of memorizing the lyrics in the *Broadman Hymnal* in church or going berserk from boredom, it is equally true that my love of fiction and nonfiction started there. I got so weary of hearing the same old Bible stories told over and over the same old way by the same old people that I started rewriting them to suit myself. I had one fine cast of characters to work with—Noah, Jonah, Lot, Moses, Daniel, David, the Magi—and I let myself go. You think God is whimsical? You ought to see Moses gleefully dashing about with a big basket picking up fish left flapping in the mud and then staring in horror as those towering sea walls close on him like a set of whale jaws. Oh, I scrambled things up.

In school I wrote poems and stories for classmates who had assignments due, and I cannot begin to tally the number of times I wrote essays as punishment for misdoings (until my teachers concluded that they were involved in a Brer Rabbit and the briar patch situation and put an end to that).

The Monday after I graduated from high school, I was on the way to Fort Jackson, South Carolina, for basic and advanced-infantry training. The two things I wanted most in my life at that time were a woman of my own and a college education, but both required money for acquisition and maintenance.

You can imagine how little a buck private earned in those days—I realized soon enough where the term *buck* came from—but when all your living expenses are met, any revenue is cream. So, while others took off to Columbia or other points for the weekend, I stayed in the barracks and read and wrote.

I was reading modern poetry at the time, but my writing efforts focused on stories and essays, primarily pieces about what it was like growing up on Sand Road. I would write everything out in pencil on legal pads and then type it up in the company clerk's office. I have no idea what happened to all that stuff, but I suspect that when I moved out of the house midway through my second year in college, it got tossed out with my baseball cards and the rest of my leavings. I regret the loss of that material, since it would make the writing of my memoir, "Growing Up in Mississippi Poor and White but Not Quite Trash," much easier.

In the eighties I started writing a good bit of fiction, beginning with the conversions of those dramatic poems I mentioned, and I launched a column, called "Ruffin-It," in the local paper. Those columns were about everything under the sun; I'm still writing it today, and it is still about whatever I happen to stumble across. You name it, and I have written about it or will tomorrow.

At some point I realized the essay potential in the column pieces and started rewriting and fleshing them out, and before I knew it, I was placing them all over: *Alaska Quarterly Review, Boulevard, Connecticut Review, Literary Review, Michigan Quarterly Review, South Carolina Review, Southern Humanities Review, Southern Living, Southern Quarterly, Southwestern American Literature. Southern Quarterly* ran four in a row. NPR featured one.

The upshot is that the familiar essay is now my genre of choice. This will be my fourth collection, and I can easily envision four or five more before I feel that I am scraping the bottom of the barrel.

I am often asked whether the essays are true, partially true, or mostly fiction. I aver that they are, for the most part, dead-on true, though pulling from memory is always a perilous proposition. Everything that we recall is subject to distortions imposed by time and circumstance, but we do the best we can with what we have. When occasional gaps occur, we fill in with what *might* have been said or done or what we *wish* had been said or done. Events are certainly more easily chronicled with accuracy than the conversations surrounding them, simply because more of the senses are involved in imprinting the memories involving action. Again, we do the best that we can.

I don't like to take literary license in familiar essays, simply because I would be violating the basic rule of the form: that it should be true to fact. But sometimes I do stretch things a bit for the sake of art, especially when I am writing about imaginary characters, such as the Pates out in Segovia, Texas, or Buford of Buford's House of Liver on the Mississippi coast, people you will not meet in this book. Even then most of the actions and conversations are sprinkled with truth. I recall what *Houston Chronicle* columnist

Leon Hale said one time when he stood to read a piece called "Homer the Rat": "Folks, this tale starts off as truth, and it goes on that way a long time." Frankly I take a few liberties with rats in this book—I mean, the part about recording and transcribing the conversations between the male and female who trashed my office is obviously exaggerated—though most of what I write about them is true.

Sometimes common sense dictates deviation from the facts. In the title essay in this book I had to make a change to render the piece believable and to cover my butt. When the essay was first published in *South Carolina Review* many years ago, here's the way the section under discussion read:

> "What do you do in Waco?" I finally managed to break in. George was holding his breath to keep from guffawing. His face looked like a brake light.
>
> "Make artificial limbs."
>
> I met George's look. "You mean arms and—"
>
> "Arms and legs, stuff like that. Yep. Been doing it for twenty years."
>
> "Uh—" I started, but I just couldn't think of anything reasonable to ask.

I changed his profession to undertaker's assistant, simply because nobody would believe that he made *prostheses!* That would have fit too neatly into the Flannery O'Connor context. He actually *did* make artificial limbs—of this I am certain, since he couldn't possibly have known how to serve up that big a dump-truck load of irony—but you talking about fact being stranger than fiction. . . .

Furthermore, what if the guy is still alive and somebody put this book in his face and said, "Look what this Ruffin guy had to say about you!" Do you know how far Ben Hur is from my house? A short chariot ride away, I'd say. "But what about this preface?" you ask. "Aren't you worried about that?" Nope: Nobody reads prefaces.

Tinny rate, I hope that you enjoy this trip. It certainly was a pleasure laying it out for you.

Acknowledgments

Parts of this book were published initially, in some cases under different titles, in the following sources:

"The Bowhunter Asks for My Bladder," *Pembroke Magazine*
"The Boy Who Spoke in Hymns," *Langdon Review*
"Dobber's Lighter," *Shenandoah: The Washington and Lee University Review*
"The Girl in the Clean, Well-Lighted Place," *Pleiades*
"The Lady with the Quick Simile," *Southern Quarterly*
"Making a Dam in Segovia," *Southwestern American Literature*
"The Mosquito," *Alabama Literary Review*
"Naming the Mussels," *Concho River Review*
"Hi-Ho, Hi-Ho, Off to the Gunshow We Go . . . ," *Literary Review*
"Rats!" *Louisiana Literature*
"Tight-Rope Walker," *Southern Living*
"To San Juan and Back," *Boulevard*
"Trains," *Southern Humanities Review*
"Travels with George, in Search of Ben Hur," *South Carolina Review*
"Workshopping a Cowboy Poem," *Southwestern American Literature*
"The Worst Drink of My Life," *Langdon Review*

Much of the material here appeared in my column, "Ruffin-It," in the *Huntsville Item.*

I would like to thank my dear Amber for the hours she put into proofing this book. I certainly thank Linda Fogle of the University of South Carolina Press for her faith in the collection.

Things Literary,
More or Less

Travels with George in Search of Ben Hur

When the late, great George Garrett came out to Texas one April a few years back to do a little reading tour, I got to go along, not because it had really been planned that way but because the benevolent deities assisted in arranging it. Originally the plan had been for George to come out for a roast of our dear friend Eddie Weems—a Texas writer who has a book on the devastating Galveston hurricane of 1900 and the great Waco tornado, books about Indians, etc.—but Eddie begged off because he said he had recently had an operation on his leg and just didn't feel like standing before a crowd and making fools of a bunch of guys who were trying to make a fool of him. In a way I was glad that it didn't work out, because Eddie was a force to be reckoned with, every bit as bad as a Galveston hurricane or a Waco tornado, and he would have pissed a lot of people off.

At any rate, Baylor was to be in on the roast, so the English Department there asked me whether, since George was willing to come out for a roast of Eddie Weems—whom they didn't particularly like because he often laughed at the way they thought and did things—wouldn't he be just as willing to come out and help them celebrate a new endowment for poetry, to the tune of right at half a million bucks: the amount of the endowment, not George's fee. George agreed to come for slightly less than that. I set up a reading at Sam Houston State, of course, and since I already had invitations to read from my new book of stories at the University of Texas and SMU, they were delirious when I proposed that George and I read together. George liked coming out here anyway because he had Houston and Rice University connections and lots of friends at UT, and he just in general liked the state and its people, but that's how George happened to be in Texas this particular time.

Now the fact is that I really enjoyed traveling with George. He was fun. He knew everybody in the Western world worth knowing and a few in the Eastern and lots in both arenas who aren't worth knowing at all, and he had a story or two on anyone you've a mind to name. Why, his Fred Chappell stories alone could fill a thousand miles of highway. Always funny stuff. The only problem was that I couldn't keep my sunglasses on because I was wiping my eyes every five minutes, and I had to stop every hour or so and take salt tablets to replenish my sodium. Trips with George were always tear-blurred pilgrimages for me.

Well, bright and early on a Tuesday morning in April, George and I set out on our tour. My wife and the kids kissed me good-bye and hugged George, who'd been staying with us, and off we went, with my wife's last words ringing in my ears: "Y'all go on and have a good time. I trust you, George." Did you ever observe that if the old maxim "a man means only half of what he says" is true, then the parallel maxim for women must go "a woman says only half of what she means"?

My wife did not say "I trust you, George, but I don't trust Paul any farther than I can throw his two-hundred-pound-plus body," but that is precisely what she meant. Actually I hoped that she did trust me after more than twenty years of marriage, but one never knows about women. This is a blessing of many dimensions, of course, and if we men had even half the sense we profess to have, we would cultivate our own mystique. To reveal all is to invite plunder. I think that she was saying to George, "Don't let him drink too much or we might all be horribly embarrassed, and remember that this is our home state and we know lots of the people you'll be seeing." I gave her the old thumbs-up sign, which to a woman might mean anything under the sun.

Now traveling and doing readings with George was sort of like the way the novelist Allen Wier put it once: you feel like the local redneck singer getting to tag along with the Beatles or the Stones, which dated Allen as much as it did exalt George, but you get the point. I mean, George was the *show,* the main dish; you were just the warm-up, the garnish on the side. If you read *before* George, you were dead; if you read *after* him, you never were alive. So what we decided to do at SMU, our first stop on the road, was to alternate: George would read first for fifteen minutes, then I'd read for fifteen; then George, then me. This was George's gracious manner of ensuring that the audience couldn't just pretend I didn't exist. It worked out fine, so we decided to do the same staggered reading at the University of Texas the next night.

When George and I got to Austin on Wednesday and met our contact, a former creative-writing student of mine who was coordinator for the Center for Writers at UT, she slipped us a little note advising us that we had been invited to dinner at the—THE—country club with George's old friend former lieutenant governor Bill Hobby and his wife and Tom Staley and wife. (Tom directed the Harry Ransom Humanities Research Center at the university.) See, this was another advantage to traveling with George. There were all sorts of little surprises like that popping up. As I say, he knew everybody. We had the entire Austin Country Club dining room to ourselves with these dignitaries, and waiters were dipping in and out, calling Bill "Governor" and answering to his every whim. And the food and liquor were *free.* George didn't let on that it was any more or less than what he had expected.

We did our gig that night before an enthusiastic audience, which was gracious enough to applaud even for me, then partied heavily at a graduate student's house. In typical Garrett fashion, George allowed himself to be passed around among students and faculty, as content to talk to an undergraduate about the fundamentals of writing as to a humped and bespectacled professor about the current directions of American fiction. I'm not particularly good at parties. I'm shy, to begin with, but the real reason is that I let a .45 go off in the bathtub with me once and lost most of the hearing in my left ear and a little in my right. (A tub is good place to clean a gun since, if you drop the tiniest little spring or pin, you can find it—but you don't want it to go off in there, especially with the door closed.) So I just can't hear well at all in crowds. I spent most of my time standing around drinking and grinning and nodding at the faces that swam before me and trying to remember what it was like being a graduate student with nothing to your name but a VW Beetle and a new wife and being deliriously drunk on love and life and learning.

But back to George. Here was another thing you came to learn about him: he took everything in stride—nobody could rattle him. (Once at a party some poet type kept trying to get George, who had been a Golden Gloves champ, to show him some of his moves, so George finally just switched his drink to his left hand and with the swiftness of the strike of a cottonmouth threw a jab and knocked the guy over a couch. George wasn't rattled: he just demonstrated what the guy wanted to see.) We'd been drinking white wine most of the evening, but around ten or so it played out, graduate students not having the depth of stock of the Austin Country Club, and I got into some bourbon a Filipino girl had brought. I kept looking around for some wine for George but couldn't find any—he was in some sort of deep conversation with a professor and dangling his empty glass as if to say, "Paul, find something to put in here so I can continue this line of bullshit"—so I decided, hey, let's see just how cool he is. This knock-down-gorgeous Filipino girl and I hatched a plan. I went into the kitchen and ferreted out a bottle of vodka, not a label you'd know, but it wasn't cloudy and it cleared my sinuses when I sniffed it, so I poured some into an empty wine bottle and went in and filled George's glass right to the brim and stood off to the side to watch. Well, it was the prof's turn to talk, so George, looking right at him and listening intently, raised that glass to his lips, took a deep swig, and, I swear to you, never winced or blinked an eye or gave even the slightest indication that it was anything other than the finest Chablis he was drinking. Cool, the man was cool.

Another thing: you could always count on George to take care of you, no matter what. Now, we were staying in a bed-and-breakfast at the edge of campus—the Governor's Inn, one of those old homes the university bought to house guests—and it had the most amazingly complex locking system that humans could ever devise. It required a combination-number entry, plus the manipulation of a couple of little knobs and levers, necessitating sobriety and at least five fingers and both thumbs for successful entry. How a university with the federal compliance record of UT can get away with a locking system that would screen out most whole and sober people and a good 99.9 percent of the physically, mentally, or alcohol impaired, I cannot imagine. But let me tell you, George Garrett, after drinking white wine and undiluted vodka for three straight hours, did it. I simply slouched on the steps until he got us in. The last thing I remembered that early morning was looking over at my half-gallon of Seagram's squatting on the dresser like a little brown troll.

Baylor was our next stop. We rolled into Waco just after noon, our trip up having been prolonged by George's insistence that he buy the kids a couple of video tapes, I all the while protesting that what they really liked was T-shirts with the logos of schools where I read and that they were cheaper than video tapes. Even with the delay we got there in time to have fried chicken and prayer with the preachers, after which we smiled and endured a couple of hours of poetry and piety—and I say this with blessed assurance that I have many friends in the Baylor English Department. At long last the group scattered, and George and I, lost briefly in the crowd, slipped away to Harrington House, where our bags were.

Now, Harrington House is a restored Victorian home on campus—every Baptist college I've ever read at has a restored *Victorian* house on campus, whether initially built there or hauled in from God knows where (and God would know, wouldn't he?)—and it is, I'm sure, a fine place to lodge and dine, though I got the feeling when we were shown our rooms that it is not a place to party. They don't call them Victorian for nothing, you know. A cursory inspection of our rooms yielded two glaring deficiencies: there were no ice buckets and there were no glasses, only coffee cups, with coffeemakers and plenty of coffee, regular and decaf. I half expected to see a sign saying, "You may sleep here and have all the coffee you want, but by heavens you'd better not *drink!*"

"How about it, George? We have a couple of hours before you read. Want a drink?" I had bootlegged the bottle of Seagram's in one of my bags.

"Sure," he said. "But what'll we do for ice?"

"The kitchen ought to have some. Or we can drink it warm."

I could tell by his look that he didn't like that option. So we went downstairs and snooped around until we found a woman wearing an apron and asked her where the ice machine was.

"Ice machine?" she asked.

"Yes'm," I said. "We need some ice."

"You want some ice?"

I looked at George, who was stone-facing it. "Yes'm. Ice."

She just stood there staring at us. Then George apparently realized that she wanted a reason. Why would we want ice up there? Now this leads us to another Garrett attribute: the man was *quick.* "We want to soak our feet," he said and smiled and nodded. "Yes ma'am. We've been walking a lot today."

She looked at our shoes, then up at George. "You want to soak your feet?"

"Yes'm," I confirmed. "We've been walking an awful lot this week. We're from Huntsville."

I'm not sure she took that as a joke. She said, "I'll be back," and slung off through a swinging door.

In a bit she bumped the door open with her butt and spun around to face us. She was holding one of those enormous restaurant oyster buckets that you could hide a good-size feral hog in. Three, four gallons, heaped with crushed ice.

"Here you are, gentlemen, ice for your feet." There we go again: a woman says half of what she means. What she meant was, "Here you are, you damned sots, enough ice to chill your whiskey through the night and well into tomorrow, when, thank God, we'll be rid of you." She knew. I could tell by the way she looked at us as she hoisted that oyster bucket into George's arms.

We lugged our ice up the stairs and fixed our drinks—in coffee cups, mind you—and crouched low in my bedroom and drank. A veranda ran the length of the front of the house, and the windows were shielded by only the thinnest of gauze curtains, as if the proprietors were saying, "If you do sin here, we'll be *watching.*"

"What if one of them walks onto the porch and sees us, George? There's probably some sort of law against this."

"I didn't see a sign," he said.

"Ignorance of the law—" I began.

"How would they know we're not drinking *coffee?*" he asked.

"Because we're crouched on the floor with a bucket of ice between us, and because of that." I pointed to the bottle of Seagram's.

"You want to go into the *closet?*"

I thought he was making a joke, but I wasn't sure. "No," I said, "that's what *they* do."

"What could they do to us?" he asked. "The very worst would be that they would ask us to leave, and we'd just drive on home tonight or out to Eddie's house. The hell with it." I liked the way he said *home.* It sounded so clean and wholesome, humming with that "m." I wanted to be in *Huntsville.* I felt vile, like I was sneaking a drink in church.

"Don't you remember the time you left that empty whiskey bottle in the trash can of the room you were staying in up here and got the English Department into trouble? You want to bring the wrath of God down on'm again?"

"That was TCU," he said quietly, "but I don't want to cause these folks grief either."

So we retreated to the closet, but found it much too small, and settled finally in the bathroom, where we sat on the floor, our backs against the outside wall, and started our little party. I filled our cups with ice. "I hope to hell she cleaned this bucket," I said. "I'd hate to come down with seafood poisoning."

"We'll just run the mixture a little richer." George poured the whiskey in right to the brim. "Skip the water, what say?"

I took a long sip. "Uh-huh. Just right. That's strong enough to kill off the plague."

He grinned. "Or plaque, which, I might point out, is far more common these days than the plague."

George's reading went well that night, and afterward we had some drinks at a bar with a member of the English Department and Eddie Weems and retired a bit earlier than the night before. During our nightcap, again crouched down in my bathroom, we were discussing the reading, and he asked why I didn't get to read with him.

"They didn't *invite* me to is why, mainly. You know, the language in some of my stories is kinda rough, the f— word sort of thing, they'd call it. I don't think they wanted to take the chance."

"You've read here before," he said, and that was true; as a matter of fact, *we* had read there together before.

"Yeah," I said, "but that was poetry, mild stuff, about family and kids. And I felt like I was reading in Sunday School."

"You know," he said, "the Bible's got the f— word in it too. Lot of *begetting* going on in that book. They allow *it* on campus, don't they?"

"The Bible or the begetting?"

"The *Bible.*"

"George, I don't remember that the Bible uses the f— word."

"Sure it does. It's all through it. It's just the Latinate version."

I smiled and nodded. "Well, maybe the Bible can get away with it. Let's just forget about it and drink."

"All right," he said. "But I've got to start eating right and drinking less when I get home. I can't go on like this. I'm over sixty now, you know."

"And I'm over fifty. But I keep thinking about those old guys in the Bible, how much they drank and begot and all. Look how long they lived."

"Well, it's a thought," he said. "It's sure as hell a thought."

We clinked our cups together and sipped again, listening to the quiet campus across the street and watching through a crack in the bathroom curtains the distant stars that hovered serenely above.

"I remember a line from Cummings that fits this occasion," George said. He reached over and shoved the curtains aside so that we could see the stars. "I'd rather teach ten thousand stars to shine than to teach a single woman how not to dance."

"I know the poem, my friend," I said, "and that's not the way it goes. The way you put it is better."

The next day, Friday, we had breakfast with the Weemses and Maureen Creamer of Texas A&M Press, then started back to Huntsville around eleven, intending to stop for lunch at the Dairy Queen in a little place called Ben Hur, whose existence was announced by one of those little green signs on Highway 164, which leads across to I-45. We simply had to learn something about the place: I mean, Lew Wallace wasn't from there, and they sure didn't film the movie there, so whence the name? Perhaps a brief visit to the town would clear up the mystery.

There is no Dairy Queen in Ben Hur. There are no standing commercial buildings in Ben Hur. There is nothing in Ben Hur except for a grid of streets through whose age cracks the grass has sprung and an occasional squalid shack surrounded by abandoned vehicles and household garbage mounded to sufficient height to show above the waist-high Johnson grass that grows profusely everywhere.

On our first pass we saw off to our left a pile of brick rubble and a broken-down building that must have been at one time a feed store, its tin roof ridge collapsed as if some great chariot wheel had made a pass straight across it. In a matter of the length of two football fields we had soybeans on both sides of us.

"Do you suppose that was it?" George asked.

"I reckon. Let's make another pass to be sure."

I turned around and eased back and turned down the first side street we came to—we called it a street because there was some asphalt left—drove to the end of it, some three hundred yards, and broke out into cultivated land again. I swung the car into a driveway that led to an old white house where a pickup was parked and—nearer to the road—a large boat, a twenty footer or so, looking terribly out of place there. A mule stared casually at us from a little pen next to the house, while a dog yapped and lunged against his chain.

"How'd you like to hole up there for the night?" George asked.

"I reckon not."

We took another street and found more of the same: Johnson grass and dilapidated houses, some with curtains and wash hanging out behind, some obviously abandoned.

"Whatever Ben Hur was," George said a bit sadly, "it's not anymore. The good-time chariots have moved on. Why don't we just go on to Huntsville?"

"Arright. Might as well head home."

Home. There was that word again.

Just as we were turning out onto the road that led back to 164 we saw him: on the front porch of an old frame house, white once but now a weathered gray, stood a wiry little man in jeans and white T-shirt leaning against a post and smoking a cigarette.

"Whaddaya say?" I asked George.

"Let's do it."

"Reckon he's the mayor?"

"Probably. I'll bet that he won by a slim margin, though. One vote. His."

I backed the car up and turned, and we eased along until we were even with the house, a foot or so out in the street. George motioned that I had room on the shoulder to pull on over.

"I'm not losing this car in that damned Johnson grass," I said, killing the engine, "and I'm sure as hell not worried about being hit by any other traffic."

The man on the porch just stood there smoking, watching us. I powered down the window on George's side and yelled past him, "Hey, com'ere."

"You're calling him the way you would call a dog," George whispered.

"Sorry," I mumbled. I raised my voice: "Uh, sir, could we speak with you?"

He took a last drag on his cigarette, held the smoke a few seconds, exhaled, and stepped down off the porch, half his body disappearing into the sea of green that lapped against the porch and came right up to the huge oval-shaped silver buckle he wore.

"Howdy," he said, dropping a forearm onto the roof of my car and lapping his right hand over the window sill on George's side. I noticed then that he had smoked the cigarette halfway through the filter; he looked at it and lifted it to his lips again and took another drag: straight fiberglass smoke. He saw me look at the filter when he lowered his hand again.

"I like to get *all* the enjoyment outta these thangs," he said. "They ain't cheap, and them filters don't taste all that bad." Then he flicked it into the grass. When he laid his hand back on the sill I could see the dark stains where he'd smoked his cigarettes well into the filter for probably forty years. He looked like Faulkner's character Mink Snopes, nothing but leather stretched over bone, his skin the color of something that had been turning over a bed of smoking coals for a day and a half, several teeth missing, his hair slicked back. I kept getting flashes of the character from *Deliverance* who took a personal interest in Ned Beatty.

He lowered his head and grinned. "What can I do for you boys?"

George grunted, shifting in his seat. He was closest to this guy. "We were just wondering—you know, why's this place here?"

The man raised his head and looked around as if deciding whether George was talking about Ben Hur or his house.

"The town, I mean," George said. "Why's Ben Hur here?"

"Well, hell," the man said, "it's got to be *some*whur."

"At's a fact," I said, leaning toward him, "but what we want to know is why is it named Ben Hur?"

He shrugged. "Hell, I don't know. People over in Waco, where I work at, ast me that a few times. They'll ast me where I'm from and I say Ben Hur and they say 'Ben Whur?' I don't have no idear why it's called that. I just live here."

"Does it have anything to do with Lew—" But George gave me a look and I shut up. He knew as well as I did that this guy had never read or even heard of Lew Wallace or the book, so why go and bring it up?

But here was a man who really wanted to talk, had found an audience, and for the next half an hour we didn't have to ask him much of anything to keep the conversation going. We learned that he had moved into the house behind him a few years before, and the *goddamn* porch fell off of it, and he built it back, and the *goddamn* lean-to garage beside it fell down, and he just left it *laying* there, and the *goddamn* roof leaked, and he fixed it, and one night, as he put it, "I seen a goddamn rat run across the kitchen floor and jumped over and tried to stomp his goddamn ass and my foot went right through the goddamn floor to the ground." And then it was rusted gas pipes and the back porch, and on and on. We soon got the idea that he was not altogether happy with his domicile. And then we learned that his *goddamn* mower "is broke, how come the grass is so high, but I got a nigger comin' in with a cow to stake in the yard, and she'll eat it down real quick if I keep her short-roped and play it out a coupla foot a day—she'll eat it flatter'n a mower or starve to death. Fertilize it too." He motioned to the grass. "Like it needs it. . . ."

It seems, according to our man with the big buckle, that Ben Hur was once a throbbing town with three cotton gins and a post office and school and stores, but back in the 1950s a "goddamn tornader come thoo and tore it all up and they didn't figger it was worth rebuildin"—that explained the piles of bricks and remains of walls we'd seen in the Johnson grass on the way in. Now it's just a few crumbling streets and a handful of people who work in adjoining towns. I wondered if it was the same tornado that hit Waco, but I dared not ask.

"Used t'be pecans everwhur," he said, waxing nostalgic, "but the goddamn squirrels come and eat'm all up, and then goddamn fahraints come in and eat the squirrels and rabbits and just about everthang else that moved or just set still. What we countin' on now is some little bugs they developin' down at A&M, about the size of gnats, that kills them goddamn fahraints—lights on their heads and bores right into their brains and kills them little sonsabitches graveyard dead. They got'm already, only they's not enough of'm to go around."

"What do you do in Waco?" I finally managed to break in. George was holding his breath to keep from guffawing. His face was red as a brake light.

"I'm a undertaker's assistant."

I met George's look. "You—"

"Embalmin' mostly. Been doin' it for nigh onto twenty years."

"Uh—" I started, but I just couldn't think of anything reasonable to ask.

"Let me tell you about a guy we got in last week that had a heart attact and fell off of his tracture over there near Mexia. Time they found him he was stiff as a goddamn rayroad rail, with his arms stretched out over his head. And that's the way he was when we picked him up. It take'n two of us to snap him at the shoulders. . . ."

"Don't you figure we ought to be heading on to Huntsville?" George asked. I could tell that he'd heard enough.

"Yeah, we'd better." I started the car and the man stepped back. "Sure 'preciate your filling us in on Ben Hur," I said, shifting into drive.

"Well, I got—" But we were moving now and he was receding in the rearview mirror, growing smaller and smaller until he was just a speck of white against that green sea of Johnson grass.

"Straight out of Flannery O'Connor," George said as we took the back road to Groesbeck, where I knew for certain there was a Dairy Queen. "I mean, an undertaker's assistant! She'd have loved him!"

"Yep, she would've."

"How old do you suppose he is, George?"

"Dunno. Seventy? Thirty?"

"That ought to be a reasonable bracket."

"Well, hell," he said. "How can you guess that sort of thing? Tell you what, though, he's been smoked well enough that he could die right there on the side of that road and he wouldn't decompose for a decade. Probably been nipping that embalming fluid too." He grinned that grin of his. "Even the buzzards wouldn't tangle with anything that tough."

"What we should have done was drag what's left of that bottle of Seagram's out and go in and finish it off with him, really get him wound up. You talking about some tales. . . ."

George soberly studied the road in front of us. "It would have been a bad move. We'd have gotten some good stories to take back—if we'd lived. But there were probably eight others just like him crouched behind the curtains just hoping we'd do something stupid like that. *We'd* be what got finished off, and nobody'd ever find our bones in all that damned Johnson grass. This car would have petunias sprouting out the windows behind one of those houses come spring."

"I wanted to ask him what he did before he started embalming. . . ."

George studied that a few seconds. "No telling. But I'll just bet you that somewhere along the way he was known by a number—and I don't mean *serial* number."

"Yeah, he looks like he might have worn white for a while. Scrawny as he is, though, the wonder is that bars could hold him."

"Tell you one thing. . . ."

"What's that?"

He grinned big. "I've never been to a place that God damned as much as he did Ben Hur."

"Ain't it so? Ain't it so? Not much escaped God's wrath."

After that I drove on in silence.

We had a cheeseburger at the Dairy Queen in Groesbeck, where we tried to get a perspective on Ben Hur, but the old-timers gathered there had no idea why the town was named that. They did confirm that it was once a ginning town that had been flattened by a *tornader.* And they told us a fantastic story about how back decades ago a bunch of busses came into Ben Hur and picked up all the residents and took them to Dallas to see a show called *Ben Hur.*

Later, as we climbed onto the interstate and headed south, George said, "It sounded as if some sort of decree went out from Rome, told them that they would be ready to go at such and such a time on a certain date, then the busses came and took them away to Dallas to see the show, with those poor folks wondering if they'd ever see the real Ben Hur again."

"They had to mean the movie, didn't they?"

"I imagine so," he said. "I doubt that they've got a stage big enough in Dallas to wheel chariots around on."

"Are you glad we went by there?" I asked him.

"I don't know. I've been thinking about it. Maybe it would have been better just to see the sign and wonder. I mean, now we know what's there. There's a metaphor in all this somewhere." He didn't say anything else about Ben Hur. I felt like I'd been run over by a herd of unreality too.

When we got home, the kids met us at the car. They pushed past me with a "Hi, Dad" and rushed to George, smothering him with affection, as if they knew innately that here was the guy with the video tapes—all Dad ever brought home was T-shirts with the names of schools where he'd read.

The Mosquito

Fiction or familiar essay, this is not, of course, where a story ought to begin, given the current attitude toward stories set on college campuses, and it is almost suicidal to use writers and such as characters. But I've always believed, since my earliest days of poverty in rural Mississippi, that when you find something of value, no matter how you've come across it, you go ahead and pick it up and put it in your pocket and keep it, deal with the consequences later.

So there I was, a minor program participant at the Bennington Writers' Conference in the summer of 1986, sitting in an audience of probably a hundred people, listening to Herb Gold read from his new novel. George Garrett and Alan Cheuse were directly in front of me; New York photographer Miriam Berkeley was to my right; and sitting to my left was Deanna Stark (name changed to protect *my* honor), heroine of this, my true-to-life, so-help-me-God story. I don't know who the fellow was directly behind me, only that he was tall and thin and from Alpine, Texas. The rest of the people were just a blur, students and staff, some from as close as Bennington, some from as far away as California. They don't really matter to the story. You have to box things off to get a framework; outside the box anybody and anything will do.

Now, you have seen women like Deanna Stark—just to my left, remember? Sleek. I'm talking *streamlined.* Not an ounce of fat anywhere on her, unless you count the padding around her kidneys, which I don't think is fair. You can't see it, after all. You ever notice how you never find yourself thinking about beautiful women's insides? Why should you? If you took one of Deanna's kidneys and mixed it up with kidneys from a priest, a septic-tank cleaner, and your grandmother, I doubt that you'd be able to put your finger on Deanna's. Maybe but not likely. Besides, some great tragedy notwithstanding, you'll probably never have to.

All *fe*-male lean meat, and every square inch of it declaring that you'd better look quick before it changes because she won't stay like this long, like it's a butterfly stage or something, and innocence a big part of it because she hasn't lived long enough and hard enough to have tainted much. As if all of her has been headed for some sort of perfect plateau where she can't stay but a few summers. And that, friend, was the glorious state that Deanna Stark was in.

OK, you're saying, so you managed to get yourself seated beside a lovely, slender young thing that, the best you could tell, was as innocent as she was pretty. So what? It has happened lots of times to lots of fellows, and it can't be that big a deal. And if you're saying that, you'd be right, right square on target, except for a little complication. And by little, I mean, by God, little. The size of a mosquito.

Picture this now, while you're trying to figure out just what was so unusual about a middle-aged man seated beside a beautiful young woman, perhaps lusting a bit, with his wife and daughter back at off-campus housing sweltering in a rare truly hot New England summer in a fanless room and no TV. A mosquito, who must have thought himself loose in some sort of heaven of flesh, buzzed around above all those bare shoulders and arms and legs and finally selected what he judged to be the one spot of all on earth where he wanted to land—on Deanna Stark's thigh.

And picture me there, but for a couple of pieces of professional correspondence between us a complete stranger to Deanna, watching that mosquito curl in, flare, and land. And then, oh, just preening and prattling to himself, he sharpened his probe, aimed it, and jabbed. Slipped the old prod into her up to the hilt as if he'd planned it for years. You can say what you want to about the females being the only mosquitoes that bite. I swear this was a guy, and what was driving him was *lust.* And I don't mean just bloodlust.

Now what was I to do, an almost stranger, while this little bastard swelled on Deanna's blood, maybe drooling encephalitis germs or something worse? Should I reach down and wave him away? Slap him flat against her thigh? Nudge her and point so that she could dispatch him?

Any of the above? Sure. What if he disappeared while I was shooshing or squashing him or drawing her attention to her thigh? How would I explain that? My hand right at or on her lean white thigh, or my finger pointing at it—and no mosquito? How would I explain that to her? No sir. There was too much thigh there, and that silky shift sliding higher every time Deanna moved.

Hell, women know you look at what they've got out for viewing, but you don't want to get caught doing it. In some sort of pristine world that we may be destined for someday men may be able to sit beside something like that and not look at it, not contort the corners of their eye sockets and hate the fact that their noses keep them from getting a three-dimensional view, but we'll be making a few more revolutions of evolution before we're there.

They know we look, just as we know that they pick their noses and fart, but no guy with any class at all wants to get caught at it—unless of course he's out with the boys, and the wolf-pack mentality prevails, and he not only looks and whistles but wants to be seen and heard doing it. I did not want Deanna Stark to know that I had any more interest in her long, smooth thigh than I would have had in George Garrett's khaki-covered thigh.

But what about the mosquito? While I was sitting there pondering my options and Herb was going on with his reading and folks were tittering and nodding in rhythm, the mosquito was becoming turgid, tumescent. I leaned forward until my mouth was no more than a foot from Deanna's thigh and lightly blew. The mosquito's wings fluttered, but he made no motion to go, seemed indeed glad for the breeze. Move, you little sonofabitch, *move!*

The closer my face got to him, the more fascinated I became. I swear he had his two rear legs cocked out and dug in, his middle two splayed lazily to each side, and with his front two he kept a steady rubbing motion going, as if he were praying or wringing his hands in ecstasy—his whole body, except where propped up by his rear legs, rested squarely on his prod. Call me crazy. I don't care. He was at exactly the right spot for my early-forties eyes to focus on him, even in the dim light of that auditorium. An inch closer and he would have blurred; an inch farther off and I would not have been able to swear to what I saw.

I put my glasses on and slid down onto one knee and leaned forward until my nose was no more than six inches from the little sonofabitch. Deanna seemed to be caught up in the reading, and down the row everyone was listening intently to Herb; George and Alan had not noticed, I was sure, and Miriam had her open eye glued to the camera. The seat backs were high enough that the people behind were blocked from view, except for the tall guy from Alpine, who squinted at me once, then turned back toward the front.

Totally enraptured now, the mosquito was propped up on his deep-stuck prod, sides bulging, a crapulent scarlet icon poised on Deanna's pale thigh. I stared in disbelief as—and I swear to you that if I lie, my eyes are responsible, not my tongue—his head swayed back and forth on the sticker, lolled in supreme gutful torpor, as if it mattered not to him whether he ever found blood again, ever flew again, his life having come to as glorious a summit as he could have wished.

It was then that, Herb's voice having risen to a climax, the room stirring to applaud, I turned my face up toward Deanna's, saw her cold eyes cast down upon me and felt the burn of shame on my cheeks. My eyes still locked firmly to hers, I lifted my right hand from the floor and pointed dumbly to her thigh and the mosquito . . . who was not there.

There was nothing to say. I rose from my knees, nodded goodnight to her, and stumbled out to the aisle. I looked back once toward the front, where Herb was bowing and smiling, and in the brightness a dark speck, large as a housefly, rose steadily toward the lights just coming back on in the ceiling, ascended like some bad angel at dawn, driven from a night of debauchery in paradise by the mounting thunder of God.

The Lady with the Quick Simile

S*cene set.* It was many, many years ago in Mississippi, and I was young and dapper, snappily dressed in a bow tie and sports jacket of yellow, black, and red plaid, ready for the world of serious poetry. I had won my first major prize, and as I stood before that audience of poets and Jackson elite in the Senate Chamber of the Old State Capitol Building reading a sampling of my work, I recognized it as the finest moment of my obscure life. And it was good.

As I was leaving the building, a nice check in my wallet, earned by *poetry,* an elderly lady approached me, extended a hand, then cupped mine with her other, and said, "Hello. I'm Eudora Welty. I just wanted to tell you how much I enjoyed your poems—and, furthermore, that you look like a Florentine painting." It was the Blue Bell on my apple cobbler, the whipped cream on my strawberry shortcake.

Puttering along in my VW Beetle on the way back to Hattiesburg and the graduate-school hovel I lived in, I ran over and over in my head what she had said and what it meant. I remembered well the painters of the Italian Renaissance, but I recalled nothing from Michelangelo, Raphael, or Giotto that I thought I looked like. Did I resemble one of the figures in Masaccio's *Expulsion from Paradise?* Was I Castagno's *David?* I couldn't find myself in Botticelli's *Birth of Venus,* and if Miss Welty recognized me among the degenerate characters of Piero di Cosimo's *Discovery of Honey,* surely she wouldn't have said anything. Maybe I was Titian's *Man with the Glove,* or perhaps, with my long hair, I looked vaguely like Mona Lisa to her. I just couldn't make the connection, but I liked it, whatever it meant. I felt good about it, and for years to come, anytime I taught a Welty story, I recalled that day in Jackson when the grand dame of southern letters said something nice to me.

A couple of years later, I was working on a book on southern fiction—one of the many projects I started in those days and never finished—and I decided it might be nice to have an interview with Eudora Welty in it. I hadn't the foggiest notion how to go about contacting her, but someone mentioned that she was making a brief appearance at a Southern Literary Festival event in Jackson, so I thought I'd simply head her off at the pass, so to speak—play my trump card.

Well, I scoped everything out and assumed a strategic position outside the building where she was speaking and near the car she had arrived in. My wife and I, married only a couple of weeks, waited. After an hour or so Miss Welty came out through double doors, escorted by her driver and followed by a throng of groupies, whom she paid no attention to. When the driver had assisted her into the backseat, I pushed past him, leaned down, thrust out my hand, and said, "Hello, Miss Welty. I'm Paul Ruffin. You told me one time that I looked like a Florentine painting, and—"

That breathless rush was all I managed before she raised her cold blue eyes to me and said simply, "And so you do," then slammed the door in my face. I stood shoulder to shoulder with my new wife and watched as the driver got in and they drove slowly away.

"Short interview," she said.

You will agree, I think, that most things said to you may be interpreted positively or negatively, depending on how hard you work at it, and I worked at it hard over the next few weeks, concluding finally that Miss Welty was simply reinforcing her earlier opinion of me rather than brushing me off. She just had a schedule to keep. I felt good about our relationship again. For many years I felt good about it, and I told my Florentine-painting story often.

Scene set. It was twenty years after that day in Jackson, and I was on the phone with Beverly Jarrett, director of the University of Missouri Press, talking with her about a new book that George Garrett and I had put together, an anthology of contemporary southern short fiction called *That's What I Like (about the South) and Other New Southern Stories for the Nineties.* Beverly had expressed an interest in publishing the book. "This is a good lineup of writers," she said, "but shouldn't you have a few more recognizable names to go along with Bobbie Ann Mason, Bill Harrison, and Mary Lee Settle?"

"What about Eudora Welty?" I asked. "I might be able to get a story from her."

"Wonderful, but how? She's virtually inaccessible."

Then I told her my story. There was a pause on the line, then a chuckle, then Beverly's voice: "She told me one time I looked like an Easter chick."

"She told you . . . an Easter chick?"

"Yeah, I think it was the yellow coat I was wearing."

I was troubled by this news. There were now two of us in the club.

Scene set. It was 1993, a reading tour, the University of Kansas campus. I was sitting in a little foyer in the student center after lunch talking with Chester Sullivan, author of *Alligator Gar* and *Answered Prayers,* among other books. We were talking about Mississippi writers.

"Is Miz Eudora still writing?" he asked. All of us who knew her, however slightly, referred to her as "Miz Eudora."

"Don't know."

"She's gotta be in her eighties, I'd figure," Chester said. "The last time I saw her. . . ." His voice trailed off. I was barely listening anyway. I was priming, waiting for an entrance for my Eudora Welty story.

He laughed. Then, oh then: "You know, once she told me I looked like a summer sunrise."

The Florentine painting faded to black.

Now, I don't know how many writers and editors there are out there who have had Eudora Welty say nice things to them, but it is not an exclusive club. She is a kind lady and loves similes—there are, I believe, sixteen on the first page of her novel *Losing Battles*—and we cannot fault her kind habit. One time I asked D. C. Berry, at the time poet-in-residence at the University of Southern Mississippi, whether he had been around her much. "A few times," he said. When I asked whether she'd ever said anything nice to him, he shrugged and said, "Naw. She's never said a damned thing to me." So there's at least one southern writer not in the club.

I have stopped talking to people about Eudora Welty. I seldom tell my story even to students now, for fear that one of them will come by after class and say, "You know, I met her once, at a conference over in Louisiana, and she told me that I looked like an Easter sunrise in Florence." I just don't think that I could take it.

Workshopping a Cowboy Poem

The knock was loud and authoritative and persistent so—still fully dressed from the trip up—I slid off the bed and parted the curtain and beheld before my motel door, brethren and sistren, two massive men clad in western wear, from black pointed-toe boots to white cowboy hats, and they were wearing big star-shaped badges. One was a shade taller than the other, and both of them were glancing left and right.

Knowing little else to do, I eased the door open the space the security chain would allow and said nicely, "Howdy, how y'all? What can I do for you?" I forewent the line that we have all learned from television—"Have you got a warrant?"—because the only questionable thing I had with me was a flask of peppermint schnapps to soothe a sore throat.

Even before I finished, one of the burlies up and said, "Can we come in? We want to talk to you."

But let me get some background in here. I had to fly out to Midland that weekend to present a program to the Permian Basin Poetry Group for their World Poetry Day Conference. They paid me well and covered all my expenses, so I was glad to go. Besides, these things can be fun—you meet lots of new people, sell and sign a few books. And when you get home, you take the family out to a restaurant and have a big, fine meal, then announce just before you rise to leave the table: "Children, poetry paid for this meal and will cover half the insurance bill due State Farm on November 1st."

When I got to the Holiday Inn there in Midland and started to check in, the clerk couldn't find my reservation. While he was working at it, I stood there studying all these big cowboy types around me, most of them in jeans and western shirts, cowboy boots and white hats, like they were all on the same team, and some of them had badges. Looked like they had just tied up their horses out front. Only they must have left them out back, because I came through the front and would have noticed horses tied to the shrubbery.

"Who're these guys?" I whispered to the clerk.

"Oh, it's a shurfs' convention we got going on here. Shurfs and debidies from all over." He stepped back from the computer and yelled to a heavy woman in the back, "Hey, Madge, I been through it twice and I can't find Mr. Ruffin's reservation!"

After a few seconds of silence a voice came back: "Ruffin?" A long pause, then, "Oh, Larry, I know whut. Look under *poetry.* The *Poetry* Society. They brought him in here." Like I was some kind of exotic animal they'd shipped in in a cage for people to look at and poke with sticks.

Well, ol' Larry gave me this look and went back to his keyboard, and I felt the eyes of all those big men leveled at me like forty-fours.

He handed me a keycard and let me study the layout of the motel so that I would know where my room was, then turned to a big guy with boots and white hat and asked him his name. Sure enough, Larry couldn't find him in the computer either. So I just said, for the sake of a little humor, "Try looking under *poetry.*"

The Hulk was not amused. The look he gave me said simply, "How'd you like me to kick your ass all the way back to Huntsville?" I knew that I had misread part of the look, because he couldn't possibly know I was from Huntsville, but I was pretty certain of the other part.

I made it to the room all right, weaving through what must have been half the sheriffs and deputies in the state, with their wives and children, and after plopping down my bags settled onto the end of the bed to watch the weather channel for news of the cold front due in that evening. There was a hell of a dust storm going on outside.

Now back to the main story. I studied the face through the cracked door and said, "I reckon so. But are you sure you got the right room?" The wind was howling behind them.

The tall one put his face to the crack, then the other did the same. "Yep," the tall one said.

I undid the safety chain and swung the door open. "So what's this about?"

The two of them just made themselves at home—lumbered over and sat down on the edge of the bed—and I took the only chair in the room. There was a single light above me, with a simple shade, and I've got to tell you that my heart was into a sort of loping rhythm. They didn't even remove their hats.

"Tell you what it's about," the short one said. He glanced at the door, then continued. "We heard the clerk mention that you had something to do with poetry."

I was surprised at how quick my draw was. "Naw, he said *poultry.* As in chickens. I'm in the chicken binness. We got a chicken convention going on here too, you know." I turned and acted like I was blowing feathers off my sleeve.

"Hell's bells," the tall one said. "A chicken man. We mighta knowed it, Darrell."

The short one stood up. "Yeah, well, we sorry to trouble you. We was hopin' we could talk to you about poetry, but we don't care nothing about chickens, except when they're fried or barbecued. Come on, Redus."

At that I waved him back onto the bed. "So what exactly did you want to talk to me about in reference to poetry?"

The one named Redus lifted his hat and scratched his head, put his hat back on. "We write poetry, me'n Darrell here, and we was hopin' we could talk to you about it. But a chicken man don't—"

"Hey, I was joking about the chickens. You just have to be careful when people find out you're into poetry."

"Tell us about it," Darrell said.

The upshot is that they were a couple of deputy sheriffs from Laredo who were also cowboy poets, which you hear a lot about these days, and they were eager to share their art with anyone who would listen. They thought maybe I was some kind of big-caliber poetry authority, so they were especially interested in hearing my response to their work. I told them that, no, I just published a little poetry, taught it occasionally, and edited a journal and press. They said that was enough authority for them, more than they were accustomed to, and asked whether I'd listen to their poems. It was early and I didn't have anywhere to be, so I said sure, why not? This is almost always a mistake, you see, but these guys did have badges, and they were big—the guys, not the badges, which were pretty much regular size.

Here's the poem the one named Darrell started off with—he passed me a hand-printed copy of it:

> I got this cow named Molly,
> Who most of the time is jolly,
> But she hung a tit on a bob-wire fence
> And now is melancholy
> And won't give milk no more.

With the two of them sitting on my bed, I relaxed in the only chair in the room and read the poem over, twice, then asked, "Would *teat* be better than *tit* maybe?" You have to start somewhere, you know, and that seemed like as good a place as any.

"Teat?" Darrell said.

"Yeah."

"Don't nobody say *teat* for *tit* out here, unless they ain't from Texas. Where at you from anyhow?"

I cleared my throat. "Huntsville. But that's neither here nor there. Let the teat—or tit—hang for now." I shifted gears. "For a poem about a cow it's nice enough, I guess, but a little sad, and—"

"It ain't about a cow," Darrell said. "I mean, yeah, they's a cow in it, but it's deeper than that, the way poetry's s'posed to be, you know. There's a cow in it, sure, she's there, but there's a, there's a—hep me out, Redus."

"It's gettin' deep in here alright. Hell, I don't know what yer trying to say. I thought it was about a cow too. Hep *yerself.*"

I cleared my throat again. Maybe it was the dust, which was blowing like hell outside. "So you're telling me that you are making some sort of profound comment in what appears to be a casual poem about an injured cow?"

"See, Redus, that's what education does for you. The clerk told us you's a university perfesser too, which is another reason why we come by. We—I need you to hep me with this poem."

I read through the piece again. "OK, then, what exactly are you saying here? I mean, what do you intend the cow to stand for?"

"If I was a cow," Redus said, "I wouldn't stand for no foolishness like this—that's fer damn sher. Whon't we move on to one of mine?"

Darrell ignored him and leaned back on the bed and stared at the ceiling. "It is a comment on how the world has gone crazy on us, has got complicated and out of control, and how our innocence has been lost."

"Sort of like Yeats's 'Second Coming'? You know, 'Turning and turning in the widening gyre / The falcon cannot hear the falconer.'"

The two looked at each other. Then Redus said, "The only Yeats I know that writes poetry is Freddie Yeats, that runs a Firestone Store in Laredo, but I never heard nothing from him like that—then there was Maudelle Yeats, one of his cousins. . . ."

"No," I said. "This is William Butler Yeats, the Irish poet, who was writing about the dissolution of Western civilization, the coming of the Antichrist. He uses the metaphor of the falcon pulling away from the falconer to launch his poem."

"You mean like the bird?"

"Uh, yes, the bird. A falcon."

"I shoulda stayed in school," Darrell said. "It's hard writing poems when you don't know about all this stuff."

Redus snorted. "Well, I take'n a whole year of junior college, and I don't remember learning nothing like that. Dissolution, my ass. Dis solution, dat solution. Everbody's got a goddamn solution."

"Shut up, Redus. Can you rattle off that whole poem, perfesser?"

So I recited "The Second Coming" for the pair, then went through it again slowly, explaining each of the images—the Sphinx, the desert birds—then summarized what Yeats was up to. (You know, the best I could—not being a literary critic puts you at a steep disadvantage in such matters. Sometimes, if you're not a critic, you have to guess.) All the while Darrell was taking notes.

"Well," he said when I'd finished, "that's exactly what I am up to in this poem."

"Then you've got to make it clearer."

"That's fer sher," Redus chimed in.

Darrell studied a few seconds. Then: "What if I started with something like, 'Running and running in the wide pas-ture, the cow no longer hears her mas-ter'? Would that do?"

"Maybe."

"Maybe not," Redus said.

"Then worked in 'Meanness has been turnt aloose on the world, and even the frogs has drowned.' How about that?"

Redus laughed. "What the hell does that mean, that the *frogs* has drowned?"

Darrell looked at him. "It means that things are out of control, fool. If the frogs drown—"

"If all the frogs has drowned, I'd say yer right on the mark. Why not add 'And all the birds has forgot how to fly'?"

"Shut up, Redus. This here is my poem." He looked at me. "Now, perfesser, how about throwing in some circling buzzards, instead of them desert birds and falcons and stuff that Mr. Yeats talked about?"

"You gon' make'm indecent, like that guy Yeats did?" Redus asked him.

"*Indignant,*" I corrected.

"No. That'd be what they call play-jerizm. They just going to be confused is all."

Redus continued. "You mean, like they're circling counterclockwise?"

"What in the hell does that mean? Buzzards don't circle a certain way."

"They do in the Northern Hemisphere. They circle clockwise. South of the equator they go counterclockwise. It's got to do with the way the earth spins. Look it up. You could have'm going backwards."

Darrell looked at me for help, but I just shrugged. "I don't think there's anything to it, but I don't know. I do know that they can't fly backwards."

Redus sneered. "You just never seen one do it is why you say so. Or did you learn that in school too?" He was beginning to develop a pretty sharp edge.

"I figger," Darrell interrupted, "that I could end with a line like, 'And what rough bull, the dark come 'round at last, slouches to the barn for corn.' How about that? Is it OK to borry *rough* and *slouch*?"

"Works for me. I don't think that Mr. Yeats would mind," I said. "But listen, guys, I've got a meeting to be off to—" I got up and motioned toward the door.

"When you ever seen a bull *slouch*?" Redus asked him as the two of them got off the bed and headed for the door. "I seen some *rough* ones in my time but not one that *slouched*."

"Never, but it don't mean that one cain't. . . ."

Redus snatched him out of the room, and the door shut their voices off. I settled down in my chair and stared at the wall. Then a knock came and they were back, but only to thank me for my help. I shook hands with both of them and closed and chained the door and lay back on the bed, for a long while wondering about the direction buzzards circle.

Was Emily Mad or Merely Angry?

Over the years I have taught a number of courses in which I used the poetry of Emily Dickinson, one of my all-time favorite poets. One reason is, I think, that she wrote many of her poems in the hymn beat, which has always been quite familiar to me. My initial appreciation of poetry came from memorizing the lyrics of all the songs in the *Broadman Hymnal,* that tome that we used in the Assembly of God Church in which I grew up. After a while, I could rattle off a hymn-beat poem in a heartbeat, a talent that later made me a professional poet at twelve. See, when my friends in school were assigned to write a poem, they would come to me, knowing how fast I was on the draw, and pay me a dime or quarter—depending on complexity and length—to write their poems for them. But all this is beside the present point. . . .

Miss Emily, she strikes students different ways. Some view her as odd but pleasant, and most seem interested more in Emily the person than Emily the poet, this in spite of the fact that, as several students have pointed out, her poems are short and many can be sung to the tune of "Amazing Grace." Why this latter characteristic should loom large would be beyond me, but for my acceptance of the fact that most of my students come from Protestant households, as I did, and know and love the hymn beat the way they do the rhythm of their own hearts.

It is a fact that many of our poets practice eccentricity; such behavior hints at genius, whether it is there or not. Usually it isn't. Miss Emily did not practice: she *was* eccentric. A graduate student said to me one time, after we had finished analyzing a Dickinson poem titled "I felt a funeral, in my brain" (the first line of the poem—Dickinson provided no titles): "This is one of the strangest poets I've ever been exposed to. Was she simply nuts?" I do not recall my answer.

Interest in Emily Dickinson the woman and Emily Dickinson the poet has surged and waned over the past hundred years, but at no point since the

1920s has she or her poetry been in any danger of disappearing from the literature texts. Indeed, given the fact that she is universally embraced by almost every school of criticism, the prospects of her continued prominence as one of the few representative modern poets of the nineteenth century seem virtually assured. Like the Bible, her work can be interpreted almost any way that you wish to fit your particular agenda, whether you are Freudian, feminist, Marxist, or of a more conventional tribe.

One of the most controversial pieces published recently on Dickinson is psychiatrist John F. McDermott's "Emily Dickinson Revisited: A Study of Periodicity in Her Work," which appeared in the May 2001 issue of the *American Journal of Psychiatry.* After conducting a meticulous study of her letters and poetry, McDermott concludes that Dickinson suffered from a broad range of mental problems, including agoraphobia (fear of open or public places), "seasonal depression," and bipolar disorder. He bases these diagnoses on her patterns of creativity and social behavior at different times in her life.

What is unusual here is not that a psychiatrist has attempted to diagnose mental disorders in a writer long since dead—this has been done a number of times—but that McDermott rendered his analysis after applying the codes of what is referred to as the modern psychiatrist's diagnostic bible, the *DSM-IV* (*Diagnostic and Statistical Manual of Mental Disorders,* fourth edition), a complex publication listing both alphabetically and numerically all known mental disorders, complete with symptoms and diagnostic criteria. This is presumably the first time that a posthumous diagnosis has been made through the application of the codes of the *DSM.*

McDermott's conclusions have of course been discounted by feminists who prefer to believe the focus should remain on Dickinson's talent and perseverance and hard work. Why are the women always being picked on, when madness must surely have been at work in the creative production of many male artists? Why must men be portrayed as superior enough to rise above their mental problems to produce their art while the creative genius of women is the *result* of their madness? But take any random group of literary critics and have them sit in a room and discuss Emily Dickinson, and the only thing you'll find them agreeing on is the fact that Emily Dickinson is dead, and even then a couple of them will insist on DNA proof.

Doubtless this will not be the last of our writers to be psychoanalyzed through the application of the *DSM* codes. James Morris's book *DSM-IV Made Easy* lays everything out so clearly that the layman might well render his own diagnoses with a fair degree of accuracy. I recently ordered the book from Amazon and set about trying to analyze some eccentric poets I know who are still alive and writing. My conclusion is that most of them are not mad at all, only angry at and disappointed with themselves. Most are suffering from profound self-loathing—for good reason.

On the Death of Edgar Allan Poe

Back in 1996 the theory was advanced that Edgar Allan Poe, that unassailable bastion of American literature (whom even the revisionists have not attempted to defile, though they've nailed every other major male writer in this country, from Heavy Herman to Dead Ernest), died of rabies. All those notions of his perishing from alcoholism or drug overdose or some other sort of self-abuse have been superseded.

According to Dr. R. Michael Benitez, a cardiologist, Poe died in a Baltimore hospital from rabies four days after his admission. Since Dr. Benitez's office is only a block from Poe's alleged grave, within shouting distance, who would know better?

Benitez has not admitted, of course, that the guy in the grave has told him anything about this rabies angle. The good doctor is basing his diagnosis, as he should, on the symptoms associated with the case. The patient was comatose the first day of his admission to a Baltimore hospital, perspired heavily and hallucinated and yelled at imaginary companions the next day, experienced a slight recovery the following day, then lapsed into confusion and belligerence and eventually died the fourth day. Further, during his decline, the patient refused alcohol and had difficulty drinking water. Benitez and a Bangkok-based physician, Dr. Henry Wilde, argue that these are classic symptoms of rabies. (Come to think of it, I have suffered those same symptoms after dealing with my two kids on a long weekend, except that the companion I yelled at was very real and yelled back, and I didn't turn down alcohol.)

Hey, if you really accept the idea that the patient under discussion was Poe, it is easy enough to believe that he might have had rabies. He was awfully fond of black birds—ravens, vultures, condors, etc. (and recall that he is supposed to have died in Baltimore, home of the Orioles, black birds with a streak of red who had some stray genes passed along from an ancestor's chance encounter with a cardinal in St. Louis [just speculating here])—so it's quite conceivable that somewhere along the line Poe was attracted to a rabid bat on the sidewalk, picked it up, fondled it, got nipped, and developed the disease. Maybe. Maybe not. Coulda been a black cat that nailed him—he fooled around with them a lot. And there is the report, though unsubstantiated, that this mysterious patient made some remark about "the hair of the dog that bit him," which you can't just automatically dismiss as figurative. What I'm saying is that if you can swallow the notion that it was Poe who died in Baltimore, the rabies bolus is not big enough to choke on.

It's a big deal these days to make long-range diagnoses. If there's any question at all about the nature of the death of the famous, wealthy, noble, or notorious, somebody's going to come along now and again with a new theory, a fresh diagnosis. If there are no eyewitness accounts (you know, like a signed statement: "I seen the freight train run right over him—sounded just like a *tornader*—and lop his feet off onto one side of the tracks and his head off th'other") and no documented evidence, then these people leave their deaths open to interpretation. Who knows what heroic dimensions the death of Elvis might swell to in a hundred years? While all along we believed he died ignominiously while straining at a very ordinary stool, fools that we are, our grandchildren will live to learn from some persistent physician that Elvis was a CIA operative killed by a Russian spy who replaced the king's Metamucil with fine-ground Gummy Bears in orange juice, which is just as lethal to the gastrointestinal tract as quick-set cement.

But I'm getting tangential here. Let's get back to this Baltimore case, about which I have my own theory, backed by authoritative documentation. You will note that listed among the patient's symptoms is his refusal to take alcohol. That, folks, is the clincher for me. They had the wrong man. It is reported, remember, that "Poe" was wearing another man's clothes when he was found. No, he wasn't. The guy was wearing his own clothes. It just wasn't Poe inside of them. Think about it. It is a fact that Edgar Allan Poe never refused alcohol in his life.

According to a friend of mine, an American literature specialist teaching at a Kansas university, Poe saw in all this confusion at the hospital an opportunity to duck out of public view and do what he had wanted to do all his life: run a sandwich shop. This scholar, who has supportive evidence from a Miami stockbroker named Leonard Thurlo, is convinced that Poe swore off writing as a satanic enterprise, married a fourteen-year-old former prostitute named Rowena Sawshank, and spent the rest of his days in an obscure section of Chicago selling an oblong sandwich that he invented. Though the submarine sandwich is reputed to have originated in New York, and a version of it may have, the first Poe boy (later abbreviated to "po'boy") was assembled and eaten on the streets of Chicago.

Edgar Allan Poe was run over by a train in Birmingham, Alabama, on August 15, 1889, while visiting one of his children—Jethro, his youngest son, married to Ambrosia Gertrude Bierce (but this genealogy is to cross-purposes, so I'll curtail it). And he was buried in Owl Creek, Alabama, Rowena's hometown. Go there sometime and see the slab for yourself in the city cemetery. It's the one with "RIP-EAP" stamped at one end, and just below it is a trail of cat tracks where one walked across it before the cement dried.

All this is true. My friend in Kansas has the papers.

Making Preparations for the Tour

In the movie *Miss Congeniality* there is a scene in which Michael Caine, who is attempting to pass Sandra Bullock off as a beauty queen, suggests to her that she use Preparation-H to reduce the prominence of the bags under her eyes. Bullock just gives him a look as if she's saying, "You're bullshitting me." But he assures her that he's not, that it works.

I appealed to my wife, who was watching the movie with me one night, and she said simply, "Maybe it works and maybe it doesn't, but I'm not putting that stuff under *my* eyes." Well, somehow or other this issue came up in my creative-writing class a few weeks later, and a couple of my female students averred that it does indeed work, though they hastily added that they had not tried it themselves.

"It reduces the swelling," one said, and the other agreed. None of the lads had anything to say, reasoning, as they must have, that it was an arena that they did not feel comfortable in.

"So," I said, "you just squeeze that stuff out of the tube, smear it on the bags under your eyes, and the bags will go away?"

"Not completely," the first girl said, "but it'll make you look like you've unpacked."

"Unpacked?"

"The bags. They'll look like bags that have been unpacked."

"Oh, OK," I said. "A metaphor at work there. That's good."

"You can use the suppositories too," the other girl put in. "Just like a tube of lipstick. Stroke it all underneath your eyes and the bags will just about disappear completely. I mean, I haven't actually tried it myself, but. . . ."

Now, whereas I do not fully trust everything I am told by my students and almost nothing I hear in the movies, I decided that the matter needed further study. I had a book tour planned to Mississippi, specifically to Columbus and Starkville, where I have kin and many old friends and former students and teachers, etc., and I got to thinking that it might not be a bad idea to try to do something about the bags under my eyes, since it's there that I show my age more than anyplace else. I mean, these bags are not Coach or Gucci, not fashionable at all, and in the mornings and late at night they do look like they are crammed full and ready for a long trip.

So the boy thought, *Self, why not?*

Well, I went out to Walmart, where anonymity is more likely than at Walgreens, and found the aisle where that stuff is kept, sorta sidling along like a dog, you know, studying the shelves out of the corners of my eyes. It was like when I had to get, uh, *pads* for one of the ladies in the house—I want to sneak up on them, seize'm quicker than a snake striking, bury them under a case of Castrol GTX, and hope like hell nobody I know is right behind or ahead of me in the checkout line. Don't ask me to explain my aversion—I'll bet it's universal among men. At least with those things, I doubt that anyone would believe that they were for me.

I went so far as to pick a tube up and look at it, even began reading the fine print, expecting it to say, "Apply nightly beneath the eyes for bag removal," like they're going to be tossed out with the trash bags from the kitchen. Using the vernacular, it don't say *nothing* about the eyes. Hell, I know what the stuff is for—Daddy kept cords of it on hand.

So there I was holding this tube of Preparation-H when a woman I knew from the university rounded the corner of the aisle. I'll bet you that the security camera, even in slow motion, didn't pick up my hand. Don't know where the tube landed—maybe in the parking lot, I just don't care—but I'll bet she didn't even see a blur, I jettisoned it so fast, spun around, and smiled like I was passing through to the toothpaste.

I felt pretty foolish on the way out of the store, realizing how close I came to actually going through the line with a tube of that stuff, making everybody believe I had problems down *there,* when all I wanted was to shrink the bags under my eyes and make a good first impression on the folks over in Columbus and Starkville. And I felt even more foolish realizing how close I came to actually putting that stuff under my eyes.

I mean, think about it. There I'd be hugging a friend or former student and she'd say, "Time has certainly been kind to you, but what in the world is that on your face, Preparation-H? You know, that smell won't come off after repeated showering." Why, I've heard cats'll follow you around—it's got shark-liver oil or something in it, not exactly what I'd call palatable seafood, but what does a cat know?

So I went on to Mississippi with my bags packed, including those under my eyes, and nobody said anything about them, kind souls that they are over there. The Books-A-Million folks ought to be glad I resisted the temptation to experiment with P-H. (Might try mayonnaise or WD-40 sometime.) They'd have spent the entire evening chasing cats away from my table.

The Girl in the Clean, Well-Lighted Place

You are on the road on a book tour, and it's late, but not late, just past the time when you know you should have eaten—your stomach has told you so. The motel room is quiet, with things scattered about in the casual clutter of a man alone, and you really want to be anywhere but here.

It's not like you're in a strange town, since you grew up just outside it and went to school here, but things have changed in thirty years, and night has settled on you like an empty shell inside which even familiar stars cannot light the way. Towns, the people in them—they change. Have to. It's their nature. You're back for professional reasons, not because of aging and dying parents, as was the case almost a decade ago; you're back briefly, and then you'll leave again, off to other places. It's not like being in a town where everyone's a stranger and the buildings and streets are strange. You know the town, and some of the people you still know, though they're older now and off in their own worlds, and your woman, the one person you really want to be with, is not with you, though you can almost imagine her beside you, sense her with all your senses, the way you *do* a woman you are profoundly in love with. *You* are the stranger, in town for a day or two, then back on the road.

You are tired of cheeseburgers and Subways and pizza, the standard fare of the book tour—you want steak in some clean, well-lighted place, as Hemingway described a café in one of his stories. You want to sit in a room where people are enjoying food and each other's company, where children chirp and giggle and couples whisper across the table to each other and rub feet, and you want to watch and listen, for this is what you do as a writer: you sit and watch and listen and record, and if you can, you make something of it.

You drive around behind Leigh Mall, where once there was a Morrison's, but the cafeteria is gone, something else in its place, but not a place to eat, so you stop and idle, then notice across the street a sign advertising a restaurant or a bar, where a full meal might be served. You drive over there and park in front. There are many parking places to choose from—it is not a busy night.

When you enter this clean, well-lighted place, you realize that you are the only person there, with lines of silent, empty tables and booths, all dressed out for company, but no one else is there. A pleasant but quiet and empty place. A restaurant without customers.

Then there are two pleasant people before you, a man probably in his late thirties, a manager perhaps, and a teenage girl, a waitress. You tell them that above all else in this life right now you want a good steak, tenderloin or rib eye cooked medium-rare, and a nice place to eat it in, that nothing else matters.

The man tells you that they cater primarily to a lunch crowd, that the only steak they serve is a rib eye, which is certainly not a specialty, that you'd do better to go over to Old Hickory or out to the Golden Horn, where they are known for their steaks. But Old Hickory's closed on Monday nights, and the Horn is way out on 82 West, and, besides, this guy's being honest, which you find reassuring, so you say, "I'll just have your rib eye, medium-rare."

The pretty little teenage waitress escorts you to your booth, which she's allowed you to choose, a hard decision since you could sit anywhere you want to, and asks what kind of dressing you want for your salad. You tell her and sit back and think about how damned lonely it is on the road, but sometimes lonely is not bad because lonely teaches you to appreciate the things and people in your life that keep you from *being* lonely. Sometimes you like lonely, but tonight you don't. Tonight you hate it.

Then your salad is in front of you, and so is she, just across the table in the same booth. She has simply slid into the booth and she's looking at you and talking while you pour on your salad dressing and wonder whether to start eating—can you do this in front of a pretty girl who's beginning to tell you about herself, whose teeth are even and perfect, whose lips and eyes and nose are perfect, whose body you remember from before she sat down: slender, wonderfully shaped, not a woman yet but more than a girl? Then you think yes, you can, and you do, and though at first you feel funny about it, by and by you don't. It just seems natural, the way that this is happening, so you do a little talking too, between bites, asking questions and such, and suddenly you're not lonely anymore.

You learn that she's seventeen, a year younger than your daughter, and in school at Heritage Academy, and lives at Palmer Home, a local orphanage, with her two brothers, where they were moved from Texas when she was four. And by the time your steak arrives you are up-to-date on Palmer Home—

where you played a couple of times as a boy—and have heard her plans for attending the University of Alabama and studying psychology.

The manager motions her to the kitchen, and she returns with your steak, which looks better than you expected and tastes just fine. Uncertain what else to do, you offer her a bite, but she declines and goes on talking—about her life, about her boyfriend, who plays football for the high school—while you listen and cut up your steak and chew, now and again asking a question. She is incredibly beautiful, with blond hair and those perfect features and skin, and her eyes are bright and at times have a little sliver of moisture along the bottom edge, maybe tears, maybe not, but certainly a suggestion that here's someone coming at you from the heart and you don't have any choice but to listen; even if you did, that would still *be* the choice because something's going on that you don't understand but like anyway, and you are glad to be a part of it. You recall a line from a Roethke poem, about a man whispering his love over the grave of a student of his: "I, with no rights in this matter, neither father nor lover." And the beauty is that there is nothing unsavory or questionable about it, here in this clean, well-lighted place, where—to this girl across the table from you—you are neither father nor lover nor ever will be. You are just a kind-faced, soft-spoken stranger from the outer dark who is willing to sit and listen to her, only a magic season from being a woman.

All too soon the steak is gone, and she is through talking and has left the booth, so you rise and walk to the counter and pay your bill while she smiles and the manager nods.

But it cannot end here, whatever magic has been at work. You tell them to wait, as if they are going to disappear once you walk through the door, and go to your truck and get books for both of them—you cannot get them just for her, for fear that your motives will be misunderstood—and go back and sign them and hand them across the counter and thank them for whatever it is this place has done for you. You give the girl, the woman in making, a twenty-dollar tip and tell her that you hope she'll realize her dreams and that she'll enjoy the books.

Then the door closes behind you again and you are under the stars in that deep vault of heaven. When you glance back toward the restaurant, she is standing at the counter looking at the books, and you don't know anymore about life than you did before you went in, only that you're not so lonely anymore and the road doesn't seem as long.

Explaining a Poem to a Student

I'm spending a lot of time lately revising older poems for new books that will soon be coming out, so I've got poetry on my mind.

The following is a poem of mine that some student at another university got stuck with on an assignment; it was in some text or anthology that her class was using. Since it deals with a favorite theme of mine, I thought I'd pass along the poem and my response to the student's questions.

Redneck with Hair on His Back
(Denton, Texas, 1990)

Standing here in his muscle shirt at the bar,
with hair on his back and chest
and tufted like the stuff of nests
in opposing crotches
of a too familiar tree,
he is little more than an upright ape
who has learned the alphabet.
With his woman he is not gentle,
preferring her in her anxious state,
taking her when he will, and
the children fear his thundering voice.

This, God's finest creation, whose
eyebrows now have drifted from his cheekbones
like continents over time until he sees clearly
between them with his dark eyes
and reasons well behind them
in that smoking vault of the brain
where he knows what women are made for
and when to come in from the rain.

Hi, Katherine.
Sorry you got stuck with one of my poems, but I'd be delighted to address your questions.

I have always hated, with passion, men who physically and verbally abuse their women. As a matter of fact, I have a story in the *Norton Introduction to Literature* called "Lamar Loper's First Case," which focuses on a young attorney's introduction to an East Texas redneck who has severely abused his wife and child. In the story I allow the young attorney to employ rather unorthodox techniques to win this first encounter and leave the redneck a wee cowering, timorous beastie.

One evening in Denton, Texas, north of Dallas, I was with some fellow writers in a bar (after a day of conference sessions at a nearby hotel) just drinking and BSing, you know, like any other group of professionals, only we didn't look at all like anything that most people would regard as professional: jeans and T-shirts and sneakers. We fit in nicely, you see, as most southern and southwestern writers do when there's beer about and you have nowhere to be until late the next morning. There's no time or inclination for pretenses.

Well, I was into at least my third beer when I noticed this burly cretin wallow in and wedge himself between a couple of bar stools and slap his hand down and order a beer. He was wearing a muscle shirt, dirty school bus yellow, and he had hair sprouting like virulent springtime weeds from his armpits and up out of that little dip at the neck of the shirt. The hair was roughly the color of the pelt of a southern fox squirrel, which you may not be familiar with—a bit lighter than the red of fox fur might help you get the picture. The hair on his head cascaded down into the back hair and gave him the overall appearance of the kind of animal you'd be more comfortable with watching through grates or bars and throwing peanuts to.

I describe him as an upright ape who has learned the alphabet, which is the analogy that came to mind as I watched him slug his beer and laugh and brag about how he'd just put his "woman in her place," which I took to mean he had just worked her over back at the trailer he'd just come from (just my assumptions about his mastery of the alphabet and the nature of his domicile, but I'd have put heavy cash on the latter). Frankly my inclination was to see just how many beer bottles it would take to cave his skull in, but I withstood the temptation, if for no other reason than that I had to read poetry to a group at ten o'clock the next morning and preferred not to have to send a tape over from the Denton County Jail.

Instead I just wrote a poem about him. I rather liked the notion of Nature struggling to separate his eyebrows from his cheekbones over time, like continental drift, so that he could at least see how to change a set of brake pads or bait a trotline. Sometimes a good, vicious poem is almost as gratifying as a kick to the groin, especially if the person it is intended for can read. On the other hand, if I had known which truck in the parking lot was his, I would have gone into the bathroom, peed in my beer bottle, and poured the stuff down his air-intake vents so that he would suffer a long time simply for being what he was: a pure-dee (southern term there) sonofabitch (universal term here).

Well, this may be more than you asked for and a little on the blunt side, KS. Trim as you see fit. It really is a simple, straightforward poem, so you can't make a whole lot of it.

My best to you, and good luck with your project.

Paul Ruffin

Some Rare and Unusual Books

At the Texas Book Festival in Austin this year I encountered some quite unusual books. Lining shelves and laid out on tables were books on everything from aardvarks to zymurgy (the branch of chemistry that deals with the process of fermentation, a fact that everyone should know). I mean to tell you, it was simply mind-boggling to discover what Texans are writing about and Texas presses are publishing.

Now, here are three unusual books that one university press has available: *The Development of the Rudder; Ships' Bilge Pumps: A History of Their Development, 1500–1900;* and *Those Vulgar Tubes.* Of these I found the last one the most enticing. I have really never given so much as a mote of thought to the evolution of rudders or the history of bilge pumps between 1500 and 1900 (or any other time period), and I doubt that anyone reading this has, with the possible exception of former colleague Phil Parotti in the SHSU English Department, who was a naval officer and may well have had full Naval Academy courses on rudders and bilge pumps. He has never mentioned these subjects to me.

Ah, but *Those Vulgar Tubes*—now, that's a book that ought to be well worth the reading. The subtitle is *External Sanitary Accommodations aboard European Ships of the Fifteenth through Seventeenth Centuries.* We're talking *toilets* here, "the downward trunking through which effluvia was directed into the sea." *Effluvia.* Now there's a euphemism for you. Can't you just hear your wife say, "Honey, scrape that dog *effluvia* off your boot before you come in this house!"

The title *Those Vulgar Tubes* is purported to have come from a poem in which a ship's chaplain begs to use the officers' inside water closets instead of the "vulgar tubes" the common sailors were required to use. It seems an ill-suited subject for poetry, but who am I to say? As soon as I can get my hands on this book, I'll review it for you. Sounds fascinating.

In the booth of a rival university press I discovered an unusual book titled *Freshwater Mussels of Texas*—big at 8½ × 11 inches, 224 pages, with 144 color plates and 110 in black and white. Mussels may have been around in the world's fresh waters for four hundred million years, and they may have been responsible for the founding of San Angelo, but I have never known the subject of mussels to come up in any conversation I've heard since the age of thirteen or so. When I was a boy, we used to go down on the Tombigbee River near Columbus (Mississippi) and track mussels in the clear water around sandbars, and this we did for two reasons only: one, to see who had the biggest mussel when we got through—when do boys ever turn down an opportunity to compare mussels?—and two, to pry them open and use the meat as trotline bait for catfish.

I can see the potential demand for books on the mammals of Texas, on dinosaurs, insects, bats, forts, Indians, weapons, sports legends, politicians, houses of prostitution, etc., but *mussels?* The authors go into the anatomy of the mussel and discuss its natural and commercial contributions; they examine its distribution, habitat, and spawning practices (every successful book these days has a little sex in it—you can imagine how this one must sizzle). It took three men to get it done (the book, that is, not the spawning), all scientists and researchers, and you can just bet that this book was funded with federal and/or state grants. Ranking right up there with the mating process of fruit flies, it's a subject ready-made for garnering grant funds.

All right, I'm sure this book makes a contribution to the world of science, and I apologize if I appear not to be taking it seriously. It might be interesting to give it as a Christmas gift, just to see whether anyone can top the joke; or you might lay it on your coffee table and get a pool going on how long it will accumulate dust before being opened. And think about how it could prepare you for parties. You know how people are always coming up and saying, "Wow, I've just finished this really terrific book called *A Scatological Approach to the Alamo*—they've done DNA and ballistic tests and determined that Davy Crockett. . . ." You lose the big news in all that background noise, but the voice comes back strong with, "Have you read it?" Your response now can be—and it must be fast—"Finished it yesterday, found it a real *bore* (they'll never get the pun), but have you read *Freshwater Mussels of Texas?*" You'll freeze them in their tracks.

But here's a better one to try, once you've read the book. Call your family physician. Say, "Hey, Doc, can you name the fifty-two mussels?" He mumbles, then replies, "Where'd you come up with that figure? Gimme a couple of minutes to think about it and I can name *all* the muscles—and, just for your erudition, there are a hell of a lot more than fifty-two—"

Now you've got him. *Checkmate!* You say simply, "OK, name me just *three* that live in the Trinity River—take your time."

Tales from Kentucky Lawyers

In the summer of 2003 my good friend Barbara Criswell, over in Mississippi, proofed for the University of Kentucky Press a book called *Tales from Kentucky Lawyers,* and some of the stories were so outrageous that she just couldn't help sharing them with me. I mean, these were unexpurgated stories, in the words of mostly small-town lawyers involved in some of the damnedest cases you could ever imagine.

I was so entertained by the few stories Barbara sent me that I decided our class project in my graduate Editing and Publishing course last fall would be to gather all the wild and woolly and wicked stories we could from East Texas lawyers and judges. You can't seriously believe that those Kentucky chaps have run into anything zanier than our people have. Well, we didn't wrap our project up, since lots of lawyers and judges promised us stuff and didn't deliver, but it's not dead and may yet be resurrected, if for no reason other than that one of the primary players in our book is our own Judge Ernie Ernst, about whom I could probably write a book.

I'm in the process of reviewing *Tales from Kentucky Lawyers,* so I thought I'd pass along a few of the stories that I think particularly memorable.

Take this one: a young man in a rural county (as if there were any other kind in Kentucky) was charged with murdering his mother and father. We are not told precisely how the crime was committed, only that it was, leaving us to speculate that he probably used a shotgun or an axe or a chainsaw. Southerners are not typically very imaginative when they choose a weapon to kill you with. They just want the job to be done right the first time, whether it's neat or not. At any rate, this ol' boy had a really fine defense attorney representing him, so the town flocked into the courtroom to see what sort of tactic the lawyer would use in a case in which the evidence against the accused was so overwhelming that it would clearly be very difficult to generate any sympathy for him. Came the closing argument. . . .

Our famous defender of the downtrodden of this earth stood before the jury and pointed to the boy and pled: "For God's sake, have mercy on this poor *orphan.*"

Now here's another one you might like, but I'll tell you in advance that it is a little indelicate, as lots of these tales are. A man was hauled into court for being intimate (uh, *very* intimate) with a hog, there being laws on the books all over the South to discourage such behavior. The only witness to the event was a little elderly lady, who took the stand and described everything that she saw. (The book does not tell us how she phrased herself.) When she had finished and was leaving the courtroom, she paused as if she had something else to say, whereupon the judge asked her whether there was anything else she thought that the jury should know about the case. After some hesitation, she looked at the judge, then the defendant, then the jury, and declared: "Well, yer honor, I just wanted to tell them that he picked the *ugliest* hog in the lot." We are not told whether this observation helped or hurt the accused.

Though it was not established what she was charged with, a woman testifying on the witness stand was asked by the prosecutor, "Did you, or did you not, on the night of June 23 have sex with a hippie on the back of a motorcycle in a peach orchard?" After a few moments of reflection, she replied, "What was that date again?"

Sometimes an attorney can't seem to quit when he's ahead. There was this lawyer defending a man charged with maiming another chap in a barroom brawl. Specifically he was accused of biting his fellow combatant's ear off. A prosecution witness to the fight took the stand, and the attorney asked him, "Did you actually *see* him bite off the victim's ear?" The witness admitted that he did not actually observe the ear being bitten off. Here the lawyer should have stopped his questioning: he had precisely the testimony he needed. But noooooooo.

He turned to the jury and raised his arms and shouted in what was described as a "very sarcastic" voice, "Well, if you didn't see him bite the ear off, just what *did* you see?"

The witness responded, "I seen him spit it out."

There was this illiterate farm day laborer, with ten children, who ended up in court in a divorce case. The judge was an understanding man, so he tried to make things as light on the poor fellow as he could; after hearing arguments from both sides, he said to the man, "Dick, I realize that you are a poor man. I realize that you cannot pay this woman much, even though you've got a whole bunch of kids here. So, I'll tell you what I'm going to do. I estimate that you make about thirty dollars a week, so what I'm going to do is give Pearl fifteen dollars a week for support of these children."

It is reported that "Dick clapped his hands enthusiastically and said, 'Thank you, judge, thank you, and I'll try to help them a little myself.'"

I AM NOT MAKING THIS STUFF UP! IT'S IN THE BOOK!

Then there was Judge Clay, pure-dee country but also highly educated, who was known for his eccentric dress and manner in court. He'd sometimes preside wearing overalls, even without a T-shirt, and people liked to come to his court just to see what might happen. Everybody liked him, though he could be tough when he had to be, so nobody ever knew exactly where he was going to land in a given case. One hot July day in a packed courtroom, the docket typically backed up, Judge Clay summoned a country boy from the back and asked him about his case.

The judge liked to call people *Honey,* since he had this paternal nature about him, so he said to the boy, "Now, Honey, what kind of trouble have you gotten into?"

The boy's reply was, "Judge, this is an absolute travesty of justice," something he'd probably heard on TV.

The judge asked him to explain.

"Well, I was driving down Main Street, and a city policeman pulled me over. I've got the ticket right here. I've got the proof right here. They charged me with having a defective muffler."

"Well, now, Honey," the judge said, "why is this so upsetting?"

"Well, everybody who knows me knows I've had that truck for years, and it has *never* had a muffler on it. It couldn't *possibly* be defective."

Old Judge Clay cackled and slammed his hand down on the desk and declared him NOT GUILTY.

This book is just brimming with such stories.

The Boy Who Spoke in Hymns

Not far from where I grew up, there lived a family named Simmons—a father, mother, and son. The boy, Buddy, was some three years behind me in school for a while, then five, then seven. He lost ground in the educational process as time rolled on.

Thaddyus (spelled wrong, yes, but applied in good faith by his parents long before he could do anything about it) and Rose Simmons knew almost from the get-go that something was a little wrong in the head with their son, Buddy. (This was not a nickname—Thaddyus *knew* how to spell Buddy, and it was the first name that came to him the minute the midwife had the red, puckered little thing slid out on a clean sheet and he saw the proper appendage. *Bertha* was poised on his tongue if said appendage had been missing.)

Buddy did not talk until he was almost four, and then he just made little bulldozer and airplane propeller sounds, which wasn't exactly talk, but was closer to it than what he'd done before, which was mostly wailing.

"Bbbbbbbbbbbppppppppppppp," he'd go.

Then came bird sounds, really good ones, maybe better than the ones made by real birds, only it was hard to tell. He could turn a flock of blackbirds hell-bent to the south in October or have cardinals clawing at the screens. Somehow he never managed to woo mockingbirds or crows, which might in some ways be smarter than other birds, but Thaddyus and Rose didn't know about that for sure. They just saw that crows and mockingbirds wouldn't even look at Buddy, even when he cawed and chirped till he was red in the face and breathless, and in fact they flew the other way, but then who knew what he might be saying in bird talk? "Hey, you ugly, noisy black bastard, how'd you like me to kick your ass?" or "How come you can't you make up your own songs, you goofy bitch?"

Words finally came to him when he started picking up lines from hymns in church. They'd be driving back from prayer meeting or Sunday morning or evening service, and he'd break out with "Hill far way stud a old rug cross" or "Mazing Grace, how sweet they soun and save a witch like me." Thaddyus and Rose would correct him, the best they could and gently, lest they discourage a boy just stumbling across real words, which, when he did use them, might well sound like the flutter of hummingbird wings: bbbbbbbbbbbbbb pppppppppppp, and finally, if they were lucky, bbbbbbbbuuutttttterrrrrr, pppppepppppppperrrrrrrrr.

They didn't have the money to take him to any kind of doctor that might be of help, and friends and family just said he was slow and would doubtless catch on as he aged. And this he did, but barely. His first years of school were ones of deep travail for the two of them, though Buddy seemed not to be bothered by the fact that other kids called him dumb and a mute. One of his teachers reported that when they started in on him, he'd just grin and sing something such as: "When we been there ten thousand years, bright shinin' as the sun . . ." and end with an emphatic "be-*gun!*" And they'd shut up and back off, not knowing quite what to make of him. You know, like whether maybe he had some kind of religious powers and all, or perhaps that stress on *gun* might have some extra heft to it for a reason.

"It is real eerie," she told Thaddyus and Rose one day during a conference. "He seems to read OK, maybe a few months behind the other kids, but all goes in, and nothing much comes out. He just won't talk right. I know he's understanding what he's reading, because he can shake his head *yes* or *no* to my questions as good as any other child. And even when we get a regular sentence out of him, he will use the hymn beat or just use lines from hymns, whether they make any sense or not. Better that than stuttering, I say."

So it was that Thaddyus and Rose shrugged and accepted their fate. What else was there to do? Buddy would forever be locked into the hymn beat, even when he talked about the most mundane of things. "Suppose we go to town today and buy some shoes for meeeeee?" Lord, there were times he drove them to distraction. But he was their son, and they loved him and stuck with him through it all—the ribbing and laughter from the other kids and smirks and knowing nods from friends and family. I played with him twice, that I recall, but I got enough hymns in church and didn't need them while I was driving trucks and cars along dim and dusty roads underneath the house—dust is distracting enough, and him blubbering and sneezing and slinging snot everywhere and just singing his little heart out. Mother gave him Kool-Aid both times, so he seemed not at all offended to be sent home. I remember well his body swaying from side to side as he hymned his way off down Sand Road.

It seems that no matter what kind of odd wiring God does in the heads of his creatures, unless you mess with it much, everything will come out right in the end, which is reason enough for analysts to keep their prying eyes out of people's minds. The reason I say this is that I just recently got a postcard—you can *too* still get them—from Rose advising me that Buddy has just cut his third CD and is a fast-rising star in gospel music over in Georgia somewhere, and he's writing lyrics for four major country music stars. He just might, the best she can tell (Thaddyus having been dead over five years and unable to tell anything at all, except maybe hot from not, she says, since she's uncertain which direction he went), be knocking down six figures by this time next year. More power to him—you go with the hand you've been dealt.

Making a Dam in Segovia

Bob Winship and I are at his ranch in Segovia, Texas, an hour and a half west of San Antonio, standing on the bank above the Johnson Fork of the Llano, which cuts across the corner of his property on its way north to the Colorado.

"Guidry [that's Mike Guidry, out from Houston, who lays claim to one of Winship's hunters' cabins] put in a trotline last night, and he said the river's silted in. But it's not that." He points to the rock dam that arches two thirds of the way across to a tapering shoal. "The dam's got gaps in it."

"Something there is that doesn't love a wall," I start to say to him, then do, because he's an English teacher too—on occasion only, now that he's retired.

He picks up on the Frost allusion. "Well, two can't pass abreast through them, but there're gaps just the same."

"And apparently Nature wants the dam down."

"Maybe, but I don't," he says, "and this is my slice of river here, my stones, my time and energy, and I'm going to put it back up. Guidry's shamed me. A man can take what Nature deals him, until some man shames him into resisting, and repairing."

"Or some woman," I say. "They're much better at shaming you into doing things than men are."

I want to remind him of Emerson's "Hamatreya," a poem in which Earth mocks boastful men who claim ownership of the soil, but I let it go. Besides, this is river and stones, and maybe they're different, though I don't see how; seems to me a river's even more unclaimable than dirt since it moves away always. Maybe the stones. Maybe you can claim them since they stay pretty much where you put them until a great swell rolls them around. Whatever. Philosophy's wearisome out here, with so many things to look at and so many things to do. The water's as clear as newly Windexed glass, polished almost, and slick except where it ripples thin across the stony bottom.

"When it's like this and that's most of the time," Winship is saying as we look out across the wide, flat bed, made that way years ago when he brought in a dragline and reworked the channel, "you've got twenty-six gallons a second going under the bridge, maybe thirty when there's rain upstream."

Doesn't sound like much, I'm thinking, but then I remember how short a second is and how much twenty-six gallons of water weighs, well over a hundred pounds, and I am impressed. When you try to hold it back, you're even more impressed.

"When they were setting the pilings on the highway overpass downstream back in the fifties, they asked my grandfather to help them out by pumping all he could onto the fields, which he did, and he slowed this stream to a trickle. That was a lot of water to dump, but he did it, with that old one-cylinder engine pounding away and the eight-inch take-up pipe humming. It helped, they told him later, and they thanked him."

"And it all came back to the river," I muse. "Went down to bedrock, which isn't far, and came right back to the river."

"He slowed it down, don't you see, which is all they wanted."

But back to the dam. It's only when you try to tell twenty-six gallons of water a second that the trip it's making is interfering with something you want to do that you get a notion of exactly what you're dealing with. You can build and build the dam, but ultimately twenty-six gallons of that water is going to go on downriver every second, come hell or—you know. You may make it pause and reflect, but it will go on down, sure as sin in the inner city.

So I say to Winship, "Do you want to get down there and start repairing it now, or do you want to go have another beer and think about it some more?"

"Well, it's late," he says, "so we'll do it tomorrow, when we're fresh—early, before beer call. I want to be able to float Guidry's hat by dark. I want him to have to swim to check his lines."

So it is agreed. Tomorrow we'll rebuild the dam.

Early the next morning, while Bob is off in town running errands, my son and I slip down to the river and start on the dam, almost finishing repairs before Bob shows up. He pitches in then and flings shovels of sand and silt against the upwater wall, so that the current carries the finer aggregate in among the rocks and seals the dam even tighter.

Even at that, water spouts all along the perimeter. But before the sun is midmorning high, the level has risen until it slips around the edge of our barrier and begins to spill across the top.

"Guidry might not float his hat," Bob says, "but he'll find perilous footing toward the other bank. Hard work makes a dam after all, huh?"

"Yeah," I say, "but you still have twenty-six gallons a second going off to the Colorado."

"True, but as Mr. Pate [Bob's neighbor] would say, we *slown* it down. Everything goes off to somewhere. We could use Frost again here, Ruffin, 'West-Running Brook': We've made this river stand still and dance, but still it runs away. As Frost puts it, 'It seriously, sadly, runs away.'"

I am studying the boy balancing his way along the stones of the dam, his arms out wide in the mounting sun like something about to take flight. "'The stream of everything,' Frost says. 'And it is time, strength, tone, light, life, and love—'"

The boy has reached the other side and turned around. He comes back toward us, feeling out with his bare feet one slick boulder at a time, his eyes fixed straight ahead, while the water sings and gurgles beneath him, off to the north, off to wherever it is going.

Just Thinking about Shit

Once upon a long time ago I did a bit of in-depth research to discover which word among all those we regard as expletives (not in the syntactical sense, of course) was used most generously among our people on a day-to-day basis—that is, which was uttered most frequently in any of its possible forms. The f— word, as it is called, came in a distant second to the winner of this competition: SHIT.

From the Middle English word *shitan* comes our modern-day power-packed, multifaceted *sh-i-i-i-t-uh,* which even without much effort can be delivered with the *umph* of an Assembly of God evangelist. It, or one of its derivatives, may be used as virtually any part of speech, and it flings a wide linguistic net.

The winner of the four-letter competition almost had to come from our excremental or reproductive organs or functions, for swearing is elemental and rises from the limbic portion of the brain; hence it is bestial in origin. That is not to say that such utterances are not an improvement over action. They keep us from killing one another or tearing up everything dear to us, including our children, furniture, teeth, and knuckles. As Mark Twain once said, "When angry, count to four; when very angry, swear."

When I was a child, my parents taught me that only those incapable of speaking good English swore; I observed among my kin many who swore a lot less than they should have. In fact some of the brightest men I ever knew, some of the best educated, swore wonderfully. "A footman may swear," Jonathan Swift once wrote, "but he cannot swear like a lord. He can swear as often: but can he swear with equal delicacy, propriety, and judgment?" We must remember how beautifully Mark Twain could roll the curses off his tongue. One morning when he cut himself shaving, he raged at the face in the mirror, not noticing his dainty wife, Livvy, standing in the doorway. When he was finished blistering his image, she stepped forward and repeated, word for word, what he had said. He looked at her, a tight smile on his face. "Livvy, my dear, you have the words right, but you do not have the music."

So . . . though swearing emanates from impulses deep in our psyche, it may be ultimately subdued to the useful and the good and refined for proper exercise when the occasion demands.

The purpose of this piece is not simply to extol the virtues of proper swearing. It is to examine the depth and breadth of the use of the one word that appears most often and in more forms than any other among all the expletives we use.

An explanation for the popularity of the word *shit* lies first of course in its meaning. Taken literally, the word simply means the act or product of defecation; in short, it can be used as a verb to describe the act or as a noun to describe the product. A neighbor's dog shits on the lawn: what he has left is shit. One you may observe happening, the other you may wash down with a water hose or scoop up with a shovel or call the neighbor to do it. Both the process and the product are woefully unsavory, as anyone who has had to change diapers can aver, thus making the word describing them most suitable for swearing.

But the construction of the very word itself helps further explain its appeal: the *sh* sound, followed by that terminal *t.* The *sh* sound is the sound of steam being released—the *t* drops the gate on it. The only thing that would make it a more powerful word would be to elongate the vowel, but you'd have to add a silent *e* to do it; then it would no longer be a four-letter word. *Sheet* would have been a better spelling—hence, a more impressive pronunciation—but again it would no longer be a four-letter word, and an element of bedding had, I presume, already taken that title when *shit* first hit the fan.

A conversation with our hypothetical neighbor over his dog's act demonstrates the great range of application of the word.

You call the neighbor, and he meets you at the fence, leans across it, arms folded. "Howdy, neighbor, what the shit's happenin'?" (Translation: What is going on?)

"Your dog shit on my lawn." (Translation: Your dog defecated on my lawn.)

"How come you can't be polite and say he relieved hisself on your lawn?"

"OK, yer dog take'n a dump in my yard. Mighta been relief for him, but it ain't for me."

"No shit?" (Translation: No joke?)

"I'm not shittin'." (Translation: I'm not joking.)

"My dog? In yer yard? Are you shittin' me?" (Translation: No joke?)

"I shit you not." (Translation: I'm not joking.)

"The shit you say." (Translation: No joke?) "In yer yard? Well, ain't that some shit?" (Translation: Isn't that something?)

"Shit, yes, right there beside the begonias." (Translation: Yes indeedy. Right beside the begonias.) "You can still see it steaming—like . . . shit." (Translation: This is literal and needs no translation. It is a cool morning.)

"Shit if it ain't so," the neighbor says. (Translation: I believe that you are right.) "Now, how in the shit did that dog get out—" (Translation: By what method did my dog get out—)

"I don't give a shit how he got out." (Translation: I am not concerned about *how* he got out.) "Or how *come* he got out. It ain't shit to me." (Translation: It's of no great consequence to me why the dog got out.) "What I care about—"

Neighbor shrugs. "Shit happens." (Translation: Unpleasant things like this happen.)

"You know, you've always been a shitty neighbor." (Translation: You know, you've been difficult to live with as long as you've been my neighbor.)

"You're full of shit. I didn't say a word when that shit-ass dog of *yers* tore through my tomaters, shittin' and gettin' after a cat." (Translation: That is nonsense. I did not complain when your worthless dog ripped up my tomato vines vigorously pursuing a cat.) "Man, yer goin' apeshit over this." (Translation: You are overreacting to this problem. He might well have substituted *batshit,* equally effective.)

Neighbor's wife pokes her head out and yells at him. He snarls, "Why don't you get the shit back inside?" (Translation: Why don't you get back in the house?) He looks at you. "I've done took about all her shit I'm gon' take." (Translation: I've endured abuse from her long enough.) "Always shittin' on me." (Translation: She's always heaping abuse on me.)

"You big tubba shit" is all he hears as she slams the door. (Translation: You large container of feces. She could have used any number of reasonably synonymous terms: you *shit, shitleg, shit-sorry cretin, shithead, shit-for-brains,* etc.). She sticks her head back out and yells, "One of these days I'm gon' thowe all yer shit out in the road." (Translation: At some future time I am going to throw your clothes, toiletries, guns, etc.—or maybe your *dope*—into the street.)

"Is there some shit going on between y'all?" you ask. (Translation: Are the two of you having marital difficulties?)

"What the shit is that to you?" (Translation: What business is that of yours?)

You see a cop car turn the corner and ease up to the curb.

Neighbor whispers, "Holy shit! The cops are here." (Translation: Uh-oh! The cops are here.)

Big guy in blue gets out, walks over, hands on his hips. "Got a call there was some shit goin' on here." (Translation: We received a call indicating a domestic dispute or disturbance at this address.)

Were it anyone other than a man in blue, the neighbor would say "Bull-shit." Instead he says, "Nossiree," and flashes him a shit-eating grin. (Translation: The neighbor's grin looks like that of a man eating feces. This is a common enough expression, though I cannot, for the life of me, envision such a circumstance nor explain the origins of the expression.) "Me'n my neighbor just shootin' the shit." (Translation: My neighbor and I are simply making small talk. This means something decidedly different from *talking some shit,* which suggests a higher level of seriousness and excrement in the conversation. Remember that in this context, shit can be shallow or deep.)

The policeman grins. "Bullshit." (Translation: That is nonsense.) "But it ain't nothin' to me if y'all beat the shit out of each other." (Translation: I will not be dreadfully concerned if you pummel each other to the point of genuine hurt.) "Don't let me have to come back out here or the shit's gon' hit the fan. In other words, you boys gon' be up Shit Creek." (Translation: If I receive another call about you fellows, I am going to cause you some real grief.)

When he drives off, neighbor mumbles, "All them guys in uniforms thinks they're hot shit." (Translation: Law enforcement officers are very proud of themselves and their uniforms.) "Real shit on a stick." (Translation: Law enforcement officers are very proud of themselves and their uniforms.) "They don't none of'm know shit from Shinola, and deep down, all of'm's chicken-shit." (Translation: Most of them cannot discern feces from a popular brand of shoe polish and at heart are frightened by their own shadows.) "They're always around when you don't want'm, but yer shit out of luck when you really need one." (Translation: You are likely not to be able to summon one promptly when he is needed.)

"I wonder who called?" you ask.

"Beats the shit out of me," neighbor says. (Translation: I cannot say.) "It was probably my wife."

"Or another shitbird neighbor." (Translation: Perhaps another disagreeable neighbor called them.)

"Tell you what," Neighbor continues, "this shit-slangin' ain't gettin' us nowheres. Why don't we get our shit together and bring a bottle of Jack out here, get shit-faced, talk this shit over." (Translation: Our name calling and insults are not paying dividends. Why do we not compose ourselves, bring out a bottle of whiskey, become inebriated, and talk our difficulties over?)

OK, now here is the same story in translation:

You call the neighbor and he meets you at the fence, leans across it, arms folded. "Howdy, neighbor, what is going on?"

"Your dog defecated on my lawn.

"Why can't you be polite and say that he relieved hisself on your lawn?"

"All right, your dog relieved himself on my lawn."

"No joke?"

"I'm not joking."

"My dog? In your yard? No joke?"

"I'm not joking."

"No joke? In your yard? Isn't that something?"

"Yes indeedy. Right beside the begonias. You can still see it steaming—like feces."

"I believe that you are right. By what method did my dog get out—"

"I am not concerned about how he got out. Or *why* he got out. It's of no great consequence to me. What I care about—"

Neighbor shrugs. "Unpleasant things like this happen."

"You've been difficult to live with as long as you've been my neighbor."

"That is nonsense. I did not complain when your worthless dog ripped up my tomato vines vigorously pursuing a cat. You are overreacting to this problem."

Neighbor's wife pokes her head out and yells at him. He snarls, "Why don't you get back in the house?" Looks back at you. "I've endured abuse from her long enough. She's always heaping abuse on me."

"You large container of feces" is all he hears as she slams the door. She sticks her head back out and yells, "At some future time I am going to throw your clothes, toiletries, guns, etc.—or maybe your dope—into the street."

"Are the two of you having marital difficulties?" you ask.

"What business is that of yours?"

You see a police car turn the corner and ease up to the curb.

The neighbor whispers, "Uh-oh! The cops are here."

Big guy in blue gets out, walks over, hands on his hips. "We received a call indicating a domestic dispute or disturbance at this address."

"Nossiree," the neighbor says, flashing him a grin that looks like that of a man eating feces. My neighbor and I are simply making small talk."

The policeman grins. "That is nonsense. But I will not be dreadfully concerned if you pummel each other to the point of genuine hurt. If I receive another call about you fellows, I am going to cause you some real grief."

When he drives off, neighbor mumbles, "Law enforcement officers are very proud of themselves and their uniforms. Most of them cannot discern feces from a popular brand of shoe polish and at heart are frightened by their own shadows. You are likely not to be able to summon one promptly when he is needed."

"I wonder who called."

"I cannot say," neighbor says. It was probably my wife."

"Perhaps another disagreeable neighbor called them."

"Tell you what," Neighbor continues, "Our name-calling and insults are not paying dividends. Why do we not compose ourselves, bring out a bottle of whiskey, become inebriated, and talk our difficulties over?

Well, our two characters get together over a bottle of booze and pretty soon they are looped. By midnight they have forgotten all about dogs and defilement and lapsed into a supreme stupor as the moon rises over them. But for the wonders of the tension-relieving word *shit* and all its derivatives, they might both be lying exhausted from a boring, civilized exchange or bleeding from gunshot or hatchet wounds.

You can see from the translation that literal language is inherently more formal, but it renders a tale insipid, turgid, and stale, not worth telling or listening to. Profanity is the spice of language, the music. It enlivens; it invigorates; it adds sparkle and pizzazz; it converts the ordinary dry anecdote into literature; and it allows our delivery to be natural and spontaneous.

Oh by the way, I know that I have not touched on every application of the word *shit* here, but at least you now have a general idea of the magnificence of its range. Nothing else comes close to challenging its leadership in the colorful world of swearing.

To San Juan and Back

Ah, Youth!

> "O youth! The strength of it, the faith of it, the imagination of it! To me she was not an old rattle-trap carting about the world a lot of coal for a freight—to me she was the endeavor, the test, the trial of life. I think of her with pleasure, with affection, with regret—as you would think of someone dead you have loved. I shall never forget her. . . . Pass the bottle."
>
> Joseph Conrad, "Youth"

Who knows where they are now, those three men, well along in years then, and that more than thirty years ago—pilot and copilot and flight engineer—and living life on the very edge each time they took to the sky in planes that should long ago have been mothballed somewhere in Arizona, fit for little more than a roosting place for birds, abraded by windblown sand, and faded by the sun?

I would like to believe that their bones lie bleached high on some Andes peak or in a vast African desert, picked clean by vultures, their flesh taking the air again in the bellies of birds. But not stretched out, leavings of the worms, the narrow aluminum casing surrounding them corroded and wingless and trapped beneath the earth, never meant to go any direction but down. Oh, not these men, who wanted to fly and die flying, whether in flames or writhing metal or the deep, forgetful sea.

And where is she, that old crate of a plane that was such a joy to me? Scorched and shredded on some mountain slope or in a steamy jungle or slowly eroding away at the bottom of the sea? Oh, that she not be parked for the ages in the desert, those great engines forever silent, with nothing alive inside her but lizards and scorpions and birds and no sound about her but the ever-howling wind.

Anyone who has ever heard the thunder of the great radial engines that powered so many of our planes during WWII never forgets the sound, provided he has an ear attuned to such things, as I did and do. Whether it is a nine- or twelve- or eighteen-cylinder, I know that throaty roar and will tear myself away from whatever I am doing to see what is producing it: a single-engine AT-6, a twin B-25, or a four-engine B-17 or 24. It is a sound heard so seldom these days, when what passes over is a sleek jet, leaving an indistinct roar, if you can hear it at all, or a turbine-driven prop job, whose puny whine sounds like something at a model airplane show.

So it was, standing in a hangar at the Hattiesburg Airport that day back in the early seventies, that I heard a deep rumble and turned from the airplane I was admiring and ran outside and squinted into the western sky, from whence the sound came. And, oh God, it had to be big. That sound, that sound: like a *pair* of B-17s.

In time it came into sight, just above the pines at the end of the runway, gear down, flaps set, throttles back: a DC-6, silver with green markings. No regular approach pattern for that beast—it came straight in, as if anything would dare get in its path. It dropped fast, flared, and not a dozen feet from the end of the runway the main tires squawked, a little puff of smoke trailed from each, and then the nose wheel settled and it was down. The roar of reversed props, application of brakes, and just short of the other end it halted briefly as if to gather breath, rotated, and taxied toward the terminal.

"Oh, my God," I breathed aloud. "A DC-6, a fucking *DC-6!*"

I have loved airplanes all my life, having learned to fly in my uncle's Piper Cub at age thirteen and finally earning my pilot's license. I hung out at the local airport as often as I could and flew as often as a TA stipend would allow.

I watched the enormous plane taxi up and turn toward me, its engines finally shutting down, props spinning and slowing and coming to rest. Then the crew popped open a hatch beneath the cockpit, dropped a ladder, and the three exited, stretched, and looked about them, wondering, I suppose, what kind of desolation they had landed in. They huddled briefly, lit smokes, then headed toward the terminal building.

In a few minutes a fuel truck parked near the starboard wing, and the driver rolled out a hose and made his connection. When he was through, he moved to the port wing and finished the fueling. Meanwhile I waited and watched for the crew to return to the plane. What the hell was that big bird doing there at the Hattiesburg Podunk Airport? And where were they going?

I slowly walked over to the plane, my eyes fixed on the huge radial engines that powered it. I'd seen big planes before, jets of all sizes, but never a prop-driven beast like that. I stood before the port engines and admired those big cylinders, the power and noise they held, ready to be fired up and revved and move almost anything on earth.

A voice came from behind: "Big sumbitch, ain't it?"

I judged from the gold embroidery of his cap that he was the captain: a small, wiry man, leathery, and gray about the temples. Under sixty, I guessed, but not by much. His voice was deep, raspy.

"Yessir, it is. Uh, what are those, twelve cylinders?"

A gruff laugh. "Try *eighteen.* Two banks of nine." He grinned. "Seventy-two jugs spread across them wings. Lot of power there."

"Shiiiiut," I hissed. "Four eighteen-cylinder radials. That's a *hell* of a lot of power."

The other two crew members walked up then, both in their fifties, I figured, and with hard lives behind them. The commercial airline pilots you see when you board or disembark or just pass in the airport corridors look soft, like schoolteachers or insurance salesmen, men who have just showered and shaved and dressed in pressed uniforms for a sweet, quiet trip from one nice airport to another. These guys had had it hard somewhere along the line, maybe all the way. Rugged, weatherworn, all angles and shadow, and wearing jumpsuits. One held a cigarette between his fingers, the other dangled one from his lips.

The captain extended his hand to me. "I'm Charlie Bates. I'm the left seater. This here's my copilot." He pointed to the one with the cigarette in his mouth, who had just spoken to someone at the door of the building. "Billy Gillespie." He nodded toward the other one. "And that's my flight engineer, Keenan Cox."

"I'm Paul," I said, shaking the captain's hand and nodding at the other two. "Paul Ruffin."

"They called," the copilot said. "Ort to be here in less than half a'hour."

The captain squinted at the western sun. "I hope to hell so. I don't want to get in there too damn late to have some fun."

The engineer was walking around the plane, inspecting hinges and bolts and tires, looking for leaks or anything loose. The copilot went over and joined him at one of the sets of main tires.

Cox ran his hand across the top of one. "Them damn things ain't gon' last another year."

"Like the company gives a shit. . . ."

"Y'all just inspect and keep your comments to yourself," the captain told them. "We got compny."

I studied his face a few seconds. Then: "Y'all waiting for passengers?"

"Naw," he said. "This is a DC-6A, the cargo version. We got several truck-loads of stuff to pick up."

"And go where with?"

"San Juan."

"Puerto Rico?"

"Naw, Florida."

"Florida? There's a San Juan in Florida?"

He laughed. "Shit, naw. Of course Puerto Rico. I mean, ain't any San Juan in Florida that *I* know anything about."

"Oh, man. . . . I just can't imagine what it would be like to fly one of these big bastards off to somewhere like Puerto Rico—*or* Florida. What I wouldn't give. . . ."

Then two cargo vans rounded the terminal building and stopped a few yards from the plane.

"Well, that was quicker'n I woulda figgered," the captain said. He yelled for the other two to open the cargo doors. They scrambled up the ladder and disappeared, and in a few minutes one of the trucks was backed up close to the fuselage, with a conveyor ramp stretched from the truck to the plane. The men from the trucks started sliding boxes across the belt, and the co-pilot and engineer maneuvered them into place, beginning at the rear and working forward.

The boxes were large, probably three- or four-foot cubes, and they appeared to be plain cardboard with small labels on them, much too small for me to read. I was dying to know what they were loading.

"You just hang around airports, or what?" the captain finally asked me.

"Yessir, pretty much. I'm enrolled at Southern Mississippi, but I have this—well, what I call a charter service, which means nothing except that I fly students home and back weekends and holidays, mainly to build my hours. I charge incidental expenses and what the plane costs me. It's pretty slow, though, especially this time of year. I come out here as often as I can. I like airplanes."

"So I guess you got a license."

I started to give him a smart-ass answer, but he didn't look like the type who would be easily entertained. "Yessir."

"You fly multi-engines?"

"I've flown twins, yessir, nothing bigger."

"You seem to think that it might be fun to ride over to Puerto Rico in this thing. That right?"

"Oh, hell, *yes.* Yessir, I'd give anything to go."

He studied the unloading a few seconds. Then: "Well, it ain't no big deal, and it won't cost you nothing, but tell you what—if you ain't gotta be anywhere tonight or tomorrow, go pack you a bag and get yer ass back out here as fast as you can. If you get back before they get them boxes secured and we get this thing buttoned up, you can go with us. We got a extry seat in the cockpit. Got a coupla more trucks comin', so you got plenty of time."

Nothing more was said. I thanked him, streaked to my Beetle, hopped in, and drove back to my graduate-school hovel of an apartment, threw some things into a gym bag, and got back out there as fast as that little VW would go. I don't think I would've stopped for a cop—well maybe, but he would have had to kill me first.

By the time I had parked and dashed around the terminal building, the last truck was finishing its unloading. The captain was up in his seat. He slid open his window and told me to climb the ladder, which I did like I was running from fire, and then he motioned me to a plain metal chair mounted on a pole bolted to the floor right behind him.

"Just thowe your bag down there anywhere and strap yourself in. As soon as they get them last boxes onboard and the doors are closed, this big sumbitch is headed to San Juan."

"Yessir," I said, still trying to catch my breath. "Yes-*sir.*"

All that was a long time ago, I remember: those big engines coming to life, gathering speed down a narrow asphalt strip, the fast-approaching line of dark pines, the shudder of the great laden beast taking the air, and then the dropping of the pines down the windshield as, in exhilaration—at least to me—we rose into the sky.

I did not put on my headset, preferring to hear the heavy hammering of those seventy-two pistons out on the wings, not knowing whether I would ever be that close to them again. In a short while I leaned forward and watched the coast stretched out ahead, beyond it the Gulf, deep blue and flat as a sheet of lead.

Oh, it was fine, *fine:* the flight deck banked with instruments of every sort, switches and knobs and handles and gauges lit up like a Christmas tree, reds and greens and oranges and yellows, and that wonderful roar of the engines, the vibration, the smell of—well, of an airplane cockpit, a smell no one who's ever experienced it can forget. I watched the props beating the sky, a mere blur. Fine, it was *fine.*

Once we had crossed the coast and risen to our flight level, the captain motioned for me to put the earphones on, which I promptly did.

"We're out over the Gulf now, as you probably have noticed. We'll be flying down across Key West and on to San Juan. Hope we get in early enough to do some partying. Fine place to party, San Juan. Plenty of booze and women. . . ."

"Yessir." I didn't have a permanent woman, so that sounded good to me.

"For lack of anything else to do, would you like to learn about the plane, what all these instruments are? I know that you know some, but some you prolly don't."

"Oh, yessir, *yessir.*"

"Then unstrap yourself and kneel down between me and Billy, and we'll show you what we do, and then Keenan will show you what the flight engineer keeps track of." He pointed to the console between him and the copilot. "But be careful you don't touch none of them levers there and dump our asses into that Gulf."

"Yessir."

At that I knelt behind the console and studied the instruments as they pointed them out.

From time to time they would come to one where the needle seemed dead, leaned over on its starting peg, with not so much as a quiver, and I would ask, "Why is the needle not moving?" The captain always replied, in more or less the same words, patiently, paternally: "Because it don't *work.*" The first time he added, "Half the instruments on this thing don't work, but the important ones are duplicated, and between us there will be at least one that does."

I pointed to a larger instrument over by his left leg. "What's that, weather radar?" A needle was sweeping, but nothing was showing.

"Yeah, but it don't work neither."

"Then how do you know what you're flying into during the dark?"

"By looking for lightning," he said, "and by listening to weather reports and pi-reps—that is pilot reports . . . but you know that term."

I nodded. "So we're flying in a plane with half its instrumentation out of order and no weather radar?"

"Hell yeah, and this one's better'n most of them us cargo pilots fly for el-cheapo airlines." He turned and looked hard at me. "This ain't no passenger liner here. All the company cares about is that we get from one place to the other without crashing, which most of us has got the experience to do. We fly mostly by the seat of our pants, as they used to say about the old mail pilots. Wings and engines, wings and engines. Something to pull, and something to lift, a place to take'r off and a place to set'r down. That's all it takes. We can get it there. Hell, the old mail pilots could tell what the plane was doing by listening to wind in the guy wires or across the wings or the sound of the engine."

He swept his hand across the instrument panel. "Didn't need all this shit."

When they were finished showing me everything before them, I turned to the flight engineer, and he explained everything that he monitored, but he said that mostly he was responsible for navigation. Then I returned to my seat and pondered all this: twenty thousand feet out over the Gulf, lumbering along in an ancient plane loaded with only God knew what flying with half the instruments dead and no weather radar. Seats split, with cotton and straw spilling out, the dash with spidery cracks all over from long days in the sun, windows faded with time, the aluminum of the wings streaked with soot and oil, knobs used so long that whatever had been stamped or painted on them had been worn away, every aluminum surface of the cabin, once an olive green, burnished to bright wherever hands or arms or feet constantly touched.

And, you know what? Suddenly I felt heroic in that cabin with those three aging men, each bent to the purpose at hand: getting our precious cargo, whatever the hell it was, to San Juan. *Damn the dead instruments; damn the dead weather radar: full speed ahead!* And it was a good and splendid moment, and I knew then the exhilaration of Marlowe in Conrad's "Youth," sailing as second mate, facing the sea in a derelict old ship that leaked at every seam: "There was a touch of romance in it, something that made me love the old thing—something that appealed to my youth!"

"Son," the captain's voice came through my headset.

"Sir?"

"You wanna fly her?"

"Sir?"

"Do you want to trade places with Billy? Do you want to *fly* the plane?"

"Oh, God, yes. Yessir, *yessir.*"

He then motioned for me and the copilot to trade seats, which we did. I strapped myself in and looked over at the captain.

"All right, I'm turning it over to you. You'll have to wrestle with her a little from time to time to keep her on course and at altitude. The trim ain't what it used to be, so she'll drift off in a heartbeat."

"Have you been on autopilot?" I thought that it was a clever thing to ask. I wanted him to know that I knew about autopilot.

"Shiiiiiiit. The autopilot ain't worked on this thing in ten years." He motioned to the wheel. "You got it. She's all yours." And then he told me what heading to maintain—I already knew the altitude he wanted.

With both hands I gripped the well-worn yoke hard, whatever texture it might have had long since worn to smooth rubber. "Got it, sir."

So there I was at twenty thousand feet over the Gulf of Mexico holding the wheel of the biggest propeller-driven plane I'd ever been in. I could feel the vibration of her through my hands, and it was like a woman, alive and trembling to my touch. I knew a joy such as I had never known before, a thrill that raced through every nerve. I scanned the instruments, made sure my heading and altitude were right.

"Goose her a little," the captain said. He motioned to the four throttle handles sticking up from my side of the console.

I looked over at him. "All four?"

"Yeah, they're ganged. They'll move together. If you had to move one at a time, you'd never get them engines running at the same speed."

So I reached with my left hand, gripped the throttles, and eased them forward until he motioned for me to stop.

"Now, she might try to climb on you a little, so adjust the trim forward just a little to compensate." He pointed to the trim wheel, and I did it. The nose settled ever so slightly until we were dead level again at twenty thousand.

"You got this bitch whipped, boy."

I nodded and moved my eyes from instrument panel to wings, back and forth.

At one point I began to let her drift a little off course so that I could correct it. A little rudder, and she'd come right again.

The third time I did it, the captain said, "If you gon' jockey around, son, use the damn ailerons in conjunction with the rudder. If we had passengers on board, them in the very back would get their heads snapped plumb off. You know how to keep that ball centered." He pointed to the turn-and-bank indicator.

"Yessir, I know."

So I began coordinating the yoke with the rudder pedals the way I knew to do anyway. I was such a dumb ass, such a rookie.

The copilot leaned forward and tapped me on the shoulder. "Don't worry about it. You're just excited. I'd have snapped some heads off a few times myself. Don't do shit to them boxes though. They ain't gon' tell on you."

"What're. . . ." But I stopped myself, as much as I wanted to know what was back there. What would we be hauling to a place like that in big cardboard boxes that, the best I could tell, had nothing but little tags with numbers stamped on them?

"What're what?" the copilot came back.

"Nothing. I . . . nothing."

My mind had been on that cargo the whole trip, even before, when they were loading the boxes from those unmarked trucks. What the hell could it be? Guns and ammunition for some ragtag rebels fighting for the cause of freedom in some South American or African jungle? Shoulder-fired missile launchers? Mortars? The boxes seemed too light and small for heavy weaponry. Surveillance equipment? Some other kind of electronic equipment? Uniforms maybe? Tents? Maybe C-rations for starving rebels we were supporting?

Whatever we were hauling, I was part of the delivery team, and I had never felt prouder in my life. *God, this is the life! This is it! It can't get much better. . . .*

I don't know precisely where we were—maybe a couple of hundred miles from the southern Florida coast—when I noticed that the oil-pressure needle for engine number four had dropped a little from where the other three hovered. I pointed this out to the captain.

"Sir, number four is losing oil pressure. The outer starboard engine."

"No shit? I would have thought that number four was the inside port engine."

"Sorry, sir. Just showing off."

He studied the gauge a couple of seconds, tapped it with a finger, shrugged, then settled back in his seat and closed his eyes. When I looked back at the copilot, he shrugged too, but he didn't close his eyes. I knew that he was watching very closely what I was doing in his seat.

I leaned forward and eyeballed number four to see whether I could detect anything leaking from it. There were no streaks from the cowling on top, but I saw a ribbon of faint mist trailing out behind it. And then, suddenly, the ribbon broadened and darkened.

I spun my head and looked at the oil gauge, and it was plummeting toward the red mark.

"Holy shit, Captain. Look at it now!"

His eyes snapped open, and the copilot leaned forward.

"Goddamn oil line," he said quite calmly. He throttled back the engine and feathered it. I watched the propeller spin, then stop, its edges streamlined.

"What do we do?" I asked.

"Switch seats with Billy is the first thing. We can get along fine with three engines, but it could be a little trickier."

He patted me on the butt as I slid past him. "Don't worry about it, son. This shit happens all the time. And, by the way, you done good."

I strapped myself into the crew seat, and the copilot resumed his position. He kept looking out at the dead engine. "It may happen a lot, but you don't ever get used to it."

"Naw," the captain said, "it's always a surprise. Just too many things that can go wrong. The thing is that you never *ever* have a *pleasant* surprise flying these goddamn junkyard birds. Like the weather radar suddenly working, or them dee-funct instruments coming back to life. The main thing is that you got to be ready for any fucking thing to happen, because you know it's going to. We lose another engine, especially on that side, and we could find ourselves in trouble."

I studied the other three oil gauges—they all looked good, needles steady.

"So we're OK on three engines?" I kept looking ahead of the wing and down to that damned Gulf, which I knew we'd never survive if we had to put that plane down in it. Too fucking big. Maybe a single-engine, maybe a twin, but a four-engine mammoth? Not a chance. We'd break apart on impact.

"Do we have rafts aboard?" I asked no one in particular.

"Rafts?" the copilot came back. "Get the fuck real. All we got to float on is some flimsy-ass life preservers and them boxes back there."

"Stop it, Billy, goddamn it. We got three good engines, and we could practically *glide* to Miami. We'll land there and get that damn line fixed. Ain't no need to chanch it all the way to San Juan." He turned and looked at the copilot and then the engineer. "Y'all just settle the fuck down. Every one of us has been through this shit before, and we're still alive, and we'll get through it now. Just relax and let me get our asses to Miami. This might not be routine, but it ain't far from it."

Silence was the order of the hour in the little cabin, each of us fixed on his own thoughts of what or what might not happen. The captain radioed the Miami tower, fiddled with the instruments a bit, then banked slightly to the left.

I had no idea what the others were thinking, but my body was charged with adrenaline. My heart pounded, not from fear, not from anxiety, but from the sheer magic of the moment: twenty thousand feet above the Gulf of Mexico, maybe two hundred miles from the Florida coast and anything that might resemble an airport big enough to handle a DC-6, one dead engine, dozens of dead instruments, no weather radar, and God only knew what kind of exotic cargo behind that bulkhead at my back.

From time to time I leaned forward to study the instrument panel—the oil gauges were holding steady. Then I thought again of Marlowe sailing as second mate on that dilapidated old steamer. God, how I loved that story. I memorized long passages of it in an undergraduate American-lit class. I recalled his description of the ship: "She was about 400 tons, with a primitive windlass and wooden latches on the doors and not a bit of brass about her, and she had a big square stern. Below her name in big letters, a lot of scroll work, with the gilt off, with some sort of a coat of arms, with the motto Do or Die underneath. I remember it took my fancy immensely. There was a touch of romance in it, something that made me love the old thing—something that appealed to my youth!"

I might not have gotten all the words right, but I was close. What my mind was fixed on was that motto, *Do or Die*. "*Do or Die!*" I wanted to say to the captain. "*Full speed ahead!* Damn the dead engine and dead instruments. Damn two hours of Gulf down there. Get us to Miami!"

But I also remembered that the *Judea* never made it to Bangkok with her load of coal. The sure sign of her destiny came as they were pulled up in port after the pumps failed and they had to have leaks repaired—the rats left the ship. Ironically it was not the sea that got her, but fire. She took fire and burned gloriously. From Marlowe: "A magnificent death had come like a grace, like a gift, like a reward to that old ship at the end of her laborious days. The surrender of her weary ghost to the keeping of stars and sea was stirring like the sight of a glorious triumph."

Maybe, but I don't care to watch this thing go down into that Gulf and be swallowed by it, burning or not. What if another engine goes? How far can you make it on two, Captain? As the joke goes, all the way to the crash site. . . .

I glanced about the cabin, scarred and faded from use and neglect, leaned and looked out at the still propeller on number four, lightly quivering in the slipstream, and I studied the backs of the three gray-haired men before me, men who had known the glory of flight for so long, and a feeling of power and elation swept through me, and Marlowe's words came again: "What next? I thought. Now, this is something like. This is great. I wonder what will happen. O youth!"

Oh, Youth. Oh, beautiful Youth. It laughs in the fanged mouth of destiny; it summons its strength, its resolve, and it knows not the fear of death. There we were at twenty thousand feet in a piece of shit of a plane flying a mysterious load of something to a piece of shit of a country for some reason or other, an engine dead, the whole thing a disaster waiting to happen, and suddenly I loved every inch of her, dead engine and all, dead instruments, wired and pieced together and made to go on flying until someday she would be scattered across a mountaintop or swallowed by the sea. I just didn't want her to sit and rot in that Arizona graveyard. How unlike the sleek meticulously maintained jets leaving their trails across the sky above us, so sophisticated that a pilot had to do little more than twist a few knobs, punch a few buttons, and the plane would fly itself. Those guys never had to worry about dead instruments, about defective weather radar.

And I loved those aging men who kept her in the air, no matter what. I wanted to reach and hug them, these men who, though far from youth, still feared nothing, still pushed on through the sky. And I wondered what they were thinking about as they busied themselves with all the details necessary to get us to Miami and on concrete once again.

But I knew what the captain was thinking: *Shit, this'll delay our partying. All them women, all that booze. We'll be hours late getting to San Juan.*

So I sat back and took it all in, luxuriating in the knowledge that for the first time in my life I was engaged in something truly heroic, something of greater significance than ever before. Who knew how many lives would be impacted by our secret cargo? Maybe I was just a hitchhiker, but for a few brief, shining minutes I flew that great bird, I felt her trembling to my touch. *Ah, Youth!*

In what seemed well less than an hour, though I did not keep track of the time, I could see the Florida coast—down there it was twilight while we were still in the sun. Slowly it approached and then slid beneath us. All the while there were exchanges between Miami International and the captain. A slight bank to the right, and, after miles and miles of Florida passed under us, we entered the flight pattern and finally settled onto the runway and taxied to wherever it was the captain had been told to go.

"Well, gentlemen," he announced as he switched off the engines, "we are here. God only knows for how long. . . ."

"What do we do now?" I asked.

"They repair that damn oil line, and we wait is what," the copilot said. "But I sure as shit ain't sittin' here while it happens." He undid his belt and slid out of his seat and tapped the flight engineer on the shoulder. "Wanna go get a beer, Keen-man?"

"Fuckin' A."

He looked at the captain. "You goin' with us?"

"Shit naw. I'm keeping an eye on what they do to that engine."

"What about you?" the copilot asked, looking at me.

"I'll stay with the plane, if you don't mind, sir."

"Fine with us. But it ain't likely to go down while you're sittin' on the concrete. We'll be back in an hour or so."

"You might as well make it two," the captain said. "They won't even get the cowling off for an hour. Goddamn slugs. They'd be swarming all over a damn commercial jet, but we'll prolly get a couple of old one-arm oil-stained mechanics that keep up the baggage-loading machines. Don't leave the terminal though. When this sumbitch is fixed, we headin' out."

"We'll see you in a coupla hours, then."

They popped the door and dropped the ladder and left the cockpit to the captain and me. After all that roaring and vibrating, everything seemed eerily quiet, like a graveyard. The captain motioned for me to move to the copilot's seat.

"Sorry about all this shit. It happens . . . with a fair degree of regularity."

He hesitated and rubbed his hand across the weathered dash. "What we're flying here are planes that should have been mothballed years ago. But as long as we can get'm off the ground and to where the cargo is s'posed to go, we do it. Call it practical. Call it cheap. Call it any fucking thing you want to." Hesitation again.

"Them of us that fly these things are washouts, people that can't make it as commercial pilots with the regular airlines . . . too old, too ornery, too whatever. But, let me tell you this, boy, most of us are better pilots than them high-salary passenger jockeys. You let something bad go wrong in the cockpit with one of them, and they fucking panic and wreck the sumbitch. Let one little instrument go weird, and they're on the radio wondering what the hell to do. Lose an engine, and they go fucking bananas. Let something go wrong with one of us, and we just take over and wrestle the goddamn plane to the ground. I can land this fucking plane, big as it is, on a highway or in a pasture or where-the-fuck-ever I have to. And I can slick it down on the surface of that goddamn Gulf back there. And I could do the same thing with a jet. But not them goddamn prissy airline pilots. Naw. They rely too much on electronic guidance systems and all that sophisticated instrumentation! When they have an emergency, they usually end up crashing or ruining a jet. Pussies. That's what they are—pussies."

"Yessir," I said. "I understand what you're saying."

"I don't know whether you do or not." Then his look softened. "I apologize for gettin' so worked up. I put my ass on the line every day in these damn crates for a quarter of what they make, so sometimes it gets to me. Especially when something breaks down and cuts into my fun time."

He removed from his jacket pocket a little bottle of Jack Daniels like those that flight attendants distribute on long flights and slugged it down.

"Gonna teach you a lesson, son. Gonna show you something."

He removed another little bottle of Jack, peeled the label off of it, scraping away the last little slivers with his knife, then took a roll of electrical tape out of a side pocket, pulled about five inches off of it, and wrapped the tape around the bottle. Then he took his knife and cut through the tape and peeled off the bottom part, leaving a thin black ring around the bottle. He opened it and tilted it back and sucked on it, checked the level, then gave it a little sip. He held it before him.

"All right. You see that the whiskey's level with that little piece of tape now, right?

"Yessir."

He held the bottle forward and set it on a level place on the dash. "Watch the Jack in the bottle."

He tilted it to the left, and the whiskey rose above the line on the left.

"Now, if we were flying and the Jack done that, it would mean that we were banking left. And it would rise above the line on the right if we were banking right. If it come above the line, it would mean we were climbing, and if it dropped below it, it would mean we were nose-down. It's just a simple turn-and-bank indicator. Simple as it gets. That whiskey is one with the plane. The tape is the horizon. If you couldn't see *shit* out there, and nothing on the panel worked, you could tell the attitude of the plane by what that whiskey's doing.

"Them old mail pilots had a flashlight and their little bottle of booze with them, day or night, because clouds could screw you up worse than the dark, since at night you usually got the stars overhead and lights on the ground. The bottle was usually a medicine bottle full of whisky with a thin black line painted around the middle. When they got in trouble, they'd pop half the booze, down close to the line, balance it on the dash, and watch what was happenin' to the plane."

"That why you carry one?"

"Naw, I just like whiskey."

He handed me the bottle. "Take it with you. Call it a souvenir from the flight, or call it a turn-and-bank indicator. Whatever, it'll bring you good luck."

"Yessir. Thank you, sir."

I leaned back and slipped the bottle into my bag.

Then he fished another two bottles of whiskey out of his pocket and handed me one. "These we gon' drink."

"You drink while you're flying?"

"We ain't flyin'. We settin' on concrete."

Then: "Shit, we all do. We can get away with it. Don't nobody bother us about rules and regulations, which is why we like this kind of flying so much. The compny sure as hell don't care." He cleared his throat. "I've flown every prop-job cargo plane ever built, from the DC-3 on up to Constellations, and I've flown across just about every country in the world, hauling everything from field artillery to auto parts and chickens. And let me tell you this—I will go on flying until somebody makes me stop or I crash and burn."

After a long silence he added: "And I fly better when I'm drunk."

"What about the FAA?"

"Hell, they just pretend we don't exist. They don't bother with us unless we crash. Mainly we ignore them and they ignore us. They'd like nothin' better than to have to sift through the ashes of this damn thing for our bones. And the conclusion they'd come to about why we crashed would read something like this: 'These cowboys were flying a broken-down antique airplane in the modern world. The wonder is that they lasted this long.'"

"Jesus," I whispered, and I know that my voice was just brimming with awe and adulation, "what a life!"

"Yeah, what a life."

"That sounded so cynical," I said.

"What did?"

"The way you said that." I hesitated, then: "Why do you *do* it?"

He swiveled his head toward me, laid down his cigarette, and fixed his gaze at a point somewhere halfway between my eyes and the back of my head. "What in the fuck do you *think* we do this for?" He watched to see whether I would respond, then continued: "For the money? Shit. For the job security? Shit. For the glory? Shit!"

He picked up his cigarette and took another deep drag. "We do it because it is all we know how to do. It's our life. Cowboys punch cows; grave diggers dig graves; and plumbers plumb. It's what you figure you can do better than anything else.

"I been flying since I was in high school, and I'll be flying until something drops me out of the sky. And I ain't going to, by God, quit flying, no matter what. And if it comes to it, where they say I can't fly no more, that my heart ain't good enough, or my eyes, or whatever, I'll get in my little Piper Cherokee and fly it until I get ready to call it quits. When that time comes I'll fuel up one last time and fly out over the ocean until I run out of gas and aim the nose into the water. Let the fish eat me."

I cleared my throat and stared into the blue smoke that swirled about his head. He belched and reached down somewhere beside his seat and fished out two more little bottles of Jack. He pointed to a little cooler behind his seat.

"If you'll get out a bottle of water, we'll have something to chase this stuff with—you know, if you want to."

"Sure." So I got a bottle out and handed it to him, and he handed me one of the bottles of Jack.

We talked on awhile, sipping whiskey and water. There was so much I wanted to know about that kind of flying, something I barely knew existed. I knew about military aircraft and commercial liners and their crews—hell, I aspired to be a member of one—but I didn't know anything about pilots flying these ancient machines all over the world, hauling mysterious cargo on their clandestine flights. I mean, these guys were the only *real* pilots left. The rest were just electronic jockeys who had lost touch with actually flying a plane. All right, all right, maybe it was unfair, but that's the way I was feeling.

All the while we were talking, I could hear clunking and banging around out on the wing. Finally a mechanic yelled up, "We ort to be wrapping this thing up in another half a'hour or so. Yon't me to send somebody to round up your guys? No tellin' where they're at."

"Yeah, fyont mind," he yelled back.

He talked on awhile about the mail pilots, his real heroes, and I listened intently—they were heroes of mine too.

Then he got quiet and leaned back in his seat and stared out over the nose of the plane.

I was flat-ass feeling the whiskey, since I hadn't had anything to eat since breakfast. So I got bold.

I leaned close to him. "Listen, Captain, there's something—"

He turned to me. "Something what?"

"There's something I want to ask you . . . but I know that you probably can't tell me."

"Well, you sure as shit won't find out unless you *do* ask, will you?"

"OK, then I'll ask." I dropped my voice to a whisper. "If it's not classified information, can you tell me what we've got back there?" I pointed to the bulkhead behind us.

He looked at me a long time, and it was a poker face.

Then, finally: "What do you *think* we've got back there?"

"Well, sir, I have no idea. I'm figuring it's arms or electronic equipment, ammo, shoulder-fired missiles, C-rations. . . . I mean, that stuff came in unmarked trucks, and the boxes didn't appear to have anything written on *them.*"

"And why would we be picking up stuff like that in Hattiesburg fucking Mississippi and hauling it to Puerto Rico? And, by the way, they gonna start callin' them rations MREs, Meals Ready to Eat. Another one of them damn . . . whaddaya call'm, you know, to where the initials spell out a word?"

"Acronyms, only that's not exactly an acronym, since—"

"Whatever the hell it is. . . ."

"I just figured that it would be transferred to military planes there, and maybe flown to Africa or South America to help regimes we're backing. . . ."

"That whole cargo area, which is all there is of the fuselage except the flight deck, is jammed with boxes, front to back, side to side, floor to ceiling. Do you have any idea how much that much ammo or guns or missiles or electronic equipment or ackernyms—or whatever the fuck ever—would weigh? We couldn't get off the ground, especially off that little strip of concrete back there in Hattiesburg. Prolly pull the engines right outta the wings just trying to taxi with a load that heavy."

"So . . . then, what—"

"Whatever's in them boxes has therefore got to be pretty light, then, right?"

"Maybe electronic equipment."

"It ain't electronic equipment."

"Then . . . then, can you tell me what it is? Or is it classified information?"

He dropped his voice to a whisper. "It is not classified information."

"Then. . . ."

"What if I told you that everything that's in the boxes has a lot to do with pussy?"

"Sir?"

"Son . . . what we got back there is boxes and boxes and boxes of women's underwear."

The cockpit was so silent. The mechanics had quit and left, and there was no noise anywhere at all except for an occasional jet taking off or landing. It was like a tomb.

"Un . . . underwear? *Underwear?*"

"Yep, panties and nightgowns, robes and pajamas. And all of them will end up with pussies in'm."

"Captain, I don't understand."

"Son, there is a garment factory back there in Hattiesburg, and they make all this stuff, and we fly it to Puerto Rico, where they got real cheap labor, and the Puerto Ricans sew all that frilly shit on'm, lace and flowers and whatever else the fuck they sew on'm, and then we fly the stuff back. We used to do it on a regular basis, but they been trucking the stuff to Mexico lately. Cheaper transportation . . . labor's about the same."

"Underwear," I said softly, more to myself than to him. "Underwear."

"You disappointed?"

"Well, I'll have to admit that if I had had to list a thousand things that we might be hauling to Puerto Rico, women's underwear would not be among them."

"Don't be disappointed. Underwear's more important than guns, when you get right down to it. Everybody's got to have underwear. And just think about all the pussy that's going to be in them things back there. Thousands of pussies."

After a few minutes of silence the copilot and flight engineer showed up, and, after running that engine through its paces to be certain the oil line didn't leak, we were airborne again, aiming for San Juan and what was left of the night for women and booze.

I felt a little numb. The glory was gone out of it now. Our piece of shit of a plane, flown by three old buzzards with nothing but whiskey and women on their minds, was hauling a load of women's underwear. Not guns or ammo or electronics, nothing to help our rebel friends in some African country. Fucking *women's underwear. Ah, Youth,* my ass.

The night was wild, what was left of it, and so was the morning. We drank and flirted with women until, sometime before dawn, the captain suggested we tuck it in for a few hours before heading back to Hattiesburg. During the night trucks would fill the cargo hold with a return load of *frilled pussy palaces,* as he put it and we'd be flying it back before noon.

I had no money and no place to stay, so the captain took me underwing and supplied me with all the rum and whiskey I could drink, which was plenty, and even offered to buy me a woman for the night. I declined the woman, but I did later accept his invitation to sleep a few hours on the couch in his hotel room after he'd finished with the woman he had bought. While they were in the room I just sat outside under some palms and thought about the flight over. And about goddamn women's underwear.

He came down and found me and took me to the room just before the sky lightened, and talked briefly before crashing—you know, in the gentler sense.

The last thing I heard him say was, "Underwear ain't bad. Better'n chickens, for damn sure. Underwear . . . so much pussy. . . ."

The brief breakfast and ride to the airport were just a blur. Two minutes shy of noon we received word from the tower that we were cleared for takeoff, and the captain eased the throttles forward, and we were rolling, all four of us still soused.

"Uh, Captain," a voice came from the tower. I was in my crew seat, but I had on a headset.

We were now picking up speed—sixty, seventy, eighty. . . .

"Whut say, tower?"

"Captain, your starboard gear is on the shoulder." The voice was calm. "You need to get back on the runway."

I wondered why the takeoff seemed so rough. I looked through the windshield then, and we were almost in the grass on the right side.

"Roger." He braked slightly with the left pedal and brought the plane back to the center stripe, then braked right to straighten it, and in a few seconds we were airborne.

He glanced at me. "Motherfuckers. I should've swung on over onto the grass and took off from the median. If a jet jockey got off on the shoulder, passengers would be screaming, and his ass would get a dressing down, maybe even fired. I guarantee you that if I *had* of took off from the median, HQ would never hear about it. And even if they did, they wouldn't give a shit, long as we got back to Hattiesburg with that underwear. You never heard any boxes back there squeal, did you?"

"No, sir. I did not. They kept very quiet about it."

"Tower cocksuckers." He was slurring a little. "It's a wonder they even tell us what to do. Most of'm would just as soon see us crash and burn anyhow, except that we'd prolly take a commercial jet and two hundred passengers down with us."

"Well," the copilot broke in, "we sure don't make their lives any easier. You remember the time the radios were dead and we had to figure out how to get in here without gettin' killed?"

He turned and looked at me. "Missed a damn American Airlines 737 by a coupla hundred yards. That one scared the shit out of me."

The captain nodded. "Sure do. We almost got in trouble for that one, except that it wasn't our fault, and HQ really didn't care anyway, as long as we got *that goddamn underwear* down safely."

"And the time the hydraulics went out completely and we had to wrestle this damn thing like a bull and nearly tore up the landing gear when we hit the runway and then thought we wouldn't get'r stopped in time? The time we didn't have a pressurized cockpit and had to fly at ten thousand feet?"

"Oh yeah," said the captain. Then he looked back at me. "And that's just the tip of the ice pick, so to spick."

I remember little of the trip back. I kept looking at the backs of those gray heads—the captain, the copilot, the flight engineer—and wondering what was going on in them, what they remembered of the night and morning and whether they were feeling as bad as I was. I knew that at least the captain was still drunk, maybe all three, but I don't guess it mattered—as the captain said, he could fly as well drunk as sober. A set of wheels on the shoulder wasn't shit to me—I'd done some pretty stupid stuff in airplanes myself lots of times.

And I wondered just how many more weeks or months or years it would be before they drew the dark card and gravity took over for good. The wire they were walking was pretty damned thin and not very steady.

After we'd landed in Hattiesburg, we had some coffee in the administration building while those unmarked trucks came in and offloaded the boxes of underwear, all of it dolled up now with frills and ribbons and lace, ready for the female flesh that would fill it.

When the last truck pulled away and the copilot and flight engineer had secured the cargo doors, the captain and I shook hands, and I thanked him profusely for the ride I'd gone on, no matter that we were hauling underwear.

He smiled and said, "Everbody needs underwear. Just remember that."

And then he was up the ladder, and those big engines came to life. They taxied out and down to the end of the runway and turned into the wind, revved the radials, and lumbered down that stretch of concrete and lifted over the pines.

When their lights disappeared into a bank of low clouds in the darkening sky, swallowed as if by the sea or by time itself, I was still trembling a little—maybe from the vibration of the plane or the excitement of the trip or the booze from the night before. I was certain that I would never see them again, that enormous airplane and those three gray-haired men who flew it, those heroes of many a dream to come, but I knew where they would never die, so long as I lived. . . .

Ah, Youth. *Ah, Youth!*

On Likker and Guns

Drinking

A Truncated History

But for one wild night on the river a couple of miles from the house, I never had so much as a sip of any kind of alcoholic beverage until I got to basic training at Fort Jackson, South Carolina, where I was introduced to beer.

As a boy I had four ways of making money: At school I would write poems and stories for pay for kids who had such assignments due and win money rolling nickels (a game not played much anymore, I suspect). At home I killed rats in the chicken yard for Daddy and gathered drink bottles for the refunds I could get at Dowdle's Store. The poems usually brought a dime or a quarter, depending on length, and essays and stories were always worth at least a quarter, sometimes fifty cents. Daddy gave me a nickel for every head-shot rat and three cents for every one hit someplace other than the head. I was, then, a professional writer and hunter before the age of twelve.

But writing poetry and fiction for pay was seasonal, and often I would have long stretches of lying of the roof of the chicken house waiting for rats that never showed. Nickel rolling, a game in which a group of us boys would roll or slide nickels in the hallway to see who could get closest to the wall (a leaner always doubled the take), was fairly erratic income, and sometimes I walked away with nothing.

Picking up co-cola bottles, though. Well, that was steady revenue. Doc or J. H. Dowdle would pay me a penny (or two—I don't recall) for every bottle I brought in, so I scoured the ditches weekly along Sand Road and Highway 50, sometimes walking and collecting the bottles in a bag, sometimes riding my bike, on which I mounted a front basket expressly for hauling bottles. In a good week I could gather forty or fifty.

I admit with some small degree of shame that a few times I stole bottles from cases outside the store and sold them back. It was easy enough to do.

They kept the empties right at the corner of the store, and a windowless wall ran up to that corner. I would slip along the wall from the back of the store and reach blind around the corner and ease empties out of the wooden flats. I got caught only once, when some old man standing near the bottles saw a hand inching around to grab one. In a couple of strides he was standing over me.

"My God, boy, I thought that was some kinda big-ass snake comin' around that corner. What the hell you doin'?"

I was caught, sure as shit, so I just told him what I was up to.

He threw his head back and bellowed, then wiped his eyes and looked down at me.

"Damn, you a real bidnessman. Hell, let me help you out, boy."

He stepped around the corner and came back with two flats of bottles, both almost full.

"Help yourself. This'll save you a little time. It's payment for the laugh you give me."

I thanked him and hauled off the bottles—forty-one of them—on my bike. I stashed them for a couple of days and then cashed in. That was an easy week for me.

In time, as the pickings got leaner and leaner along Sand Road and the ditches across from the store, largely because other kids got in on the action, I began ranging farther from home, generally east out 50 toward the Alabama line, some weekends riding ten miles or more to load my basket. It was during those long excursions that I began to notice how many liquor bottles there were strewn along the highway: everything you can name, from whiskey to wine.

Mississippi was dry in those days, of course, being largely under the control of Southern Baptists and other Protestant groups, who at least on the surface vehemently opposed strong drink, dancing, and premarital sex, which might *lead* to dancing and drinking. They fought the legalization of liquor until some shrewd legislators got their heads together and issued a declaration that every penny collected from the taxation of alcohol would go to education, a concept that held up just long enough for booze to be legalized, at which time it was decided that it might be wiser for such revenues to go into the general fund—not that this should necessarily be regarded as deceit on the part of lawmakers. . . .

Until the drought ended, people in the Columbus area just drove over into Alabama to Tuscaloosa—a little over 150 miles round-trip—and bought their liquor and hauled it back home by the trunkload, taking the less-traveled Highway 50 rather than risk being intercepted by what we called the Highway Patroleum out on 82, the main link between the two cities—OK, *towns.* By the time they got back to the Mississippi line, they'd be through polishing off at least one bottle, which they would just toss into the ditch on their way in. It was these bottles I kept finding.

Now, in each bottle there remained at least those proverbial thirteen drops that no one has the time and patience to drain off, and sometimes there'd be a quarter of a bottle or more, as if whoever had been drinking from it got spooked and jettisoned it before he was finished.

Then something clicked. I started loading the liquor bottles into my basket too, and I stashed them on the trail that led from Sand Road to the Cold Hole (a spring-fed swimming hole) in a little cave formed by the roots of a tree that had been blown over. Once a week I would patiently pour the residual liquor from each bottle into a gallon vinegar jug that I stole from Mother, standing the smaller bottles on end with their necks in the larger jug opening and leaving them there until every drop had fallen. I threw the empties in the river and picked them off with my BB gun or with rocks, though some got away and rode off to the Tombigbee many miles downstream. I could just imagine some fisherman looking at those bottles bobbing past and wondering just what the hell kind of party was going on upstream.

In a few months I had amassed an astonishing two quarts or so, a potpourri of every kind of liquor imaginable: bourbon, Scotch, vodka, gin, rum, tequila, all kinds of liqueurs, white wine, red wine. You name your shot, and it was represented in that jug. Since red wine seemed to have the strongest influence on color, the concoction had a pink tint to it when I held it up to the light, and the smell was, uh, unusual. And powerful.

Now, as I said, I had not to that point in my life so much as tasted alcohol, other than what was in the Hadacol that Jimmy Densmore's grandfather kept by the case in a shed behind the house. (More than once I slugged some of it, and it did make me feel better.) Though highly tempted, I was loathe to take a sip from my jug. The unknown was lurking there, of course painted larger and darker by my folks' attitude toward strong drink. Further I kept thinking about how many sets of lips had been on all those bottles. But the alcohol. . . . Whatever, this was something that needed sharing. If I was going to die from the stuff in that jug, I wanted company.

Sometime during the summer of my thirteenth year, I guess, several of us boys had a campout down on the river, as we would occasionally do. I don't recall what other kids were along that night, whether any of the Masonic Home boys were with us or not, but there were four of us, I think. We camped out somewhere on a bluff near the shale outcropping we called Blue Rock, which jutted out in the Luxapalila fifteen or twenty feet. It was one of our favorite swimming holes, and the shale bulwark was a fine place to sun and frolic and eat stolen watermelons on (floated down from fields upstream) and in general do what boys do on a river.

It was a warm, still night, with a full moon, and we early on built a fire and cooked pork and beans in their cans and ate them with our fingers when they'd cooled enough and sopped the cans with loaf bread when we were through. This was the way that cowboys sometimes ate them in the movies, and it was *fine.* Then we swam awhile in the river and went back to the fire and lay around joking and talking about girls. This was not camping the way most people would imagine it. No sleeping bags, no tents, no ice chests, no Coleman lanterns or stoves, no entertainment of any sort. This was white-trash camping, the only kind I knew. After a bit I told the others that I had to go check on my set hooks, which I usually kept several of jammed in the banks—I hadn't baited them in weeks. Nope. It wasn't catfish that I had on my mind.

I made my way down the dark path that led to the Cold Hole road, thence to the cave where my stash lay hidden. I had decided that tonight was the night that I would drink from that jug, and if the stuff killed me, I wouldn't die alone.

In a while I was back with my jug, which I dramatically held before the fire and then set in front of the others, who *ooohed* and *ahhhed* and marveled mightily at this miracle that had come to pass. I felt the way Prometheus must have felt bringing his gift to mankind, only I was bringing a different kind of fire. To my knowledge, none of us had tasted liquor before. I held the jug up and looked at the fire and the faces of the others through that pinkish liquid and noted how contorted everything was, then uncapped it and tilted it back and held my breath and took two deep swallows. Then the fire was inside my throat and fast dropping into my stomach, where it formed into a hot pool, and within what seemed like a matter of seconds, even before I could get my breath and begin to taste what I had swallowed, little tentacles of warmth began radiating out to my extremities.

"*Shoooooooeeeeeeeeeeee!*" was all I could manage past my scorched tongue. I could not imagine what there was more of in the mix, but it was mostly the strong stuff.

I held the jug up and looked at the fire and the others through the liquid again, and they were even more contorted, and I figured that I might as well hit it a second time while I was still cauterized and still clutching the jug, so I took two more swallows, then leaned and yielded it to whoever was on my right.

Round and round it went, that big communal jug, and our party got wilder and louder and funnier, and the world began to spin totally out of control. Somebody suggested going swimming again, but I was on my back and couldn't even get up, could just barely roll my head toward the others. The sparks from the fire sprang up into the stars, and the stars fell into the fire, and I was seeing six boys instead of three and two moons instead of one. After a few more swallows, which I managed to prop myself up for, everything went as black in my head as those night woods.

I don't know that I have ever felt as bad as I did when the world came back into focus, if barely, the next morning. I needed to throw up but couldn't, needed to walk but couldn't, needed to pee but couldn't, needed water bad. Across the ashes of the campfire I could see three bodies, or blankets that appeared to have bodies in them, but I couldn't tell whether they were alive or dead. I was somewhere in between. The empty jug lay on its side near the edge of the ashes. I despised the sight of it.

In time I came enough to my senses to realize that I had to be home in time to get ready for church, it being a Sunday morning, a fact that came around ever so slowly in my waking head. So I struggled to my feet, crawled down to the river and had a long drink, then wadded up my blanket and tucked it under my arm and started home.

I knew the way, but the way was much longer and harder than it ever had been before, and every step was agony. Lord, I was suffering. My head was a bass drum, and every time my pulse hammered it, I saw flashes. My throat burned; my stomach burned; my *soul* burned. What Prometheus suffered when Zeus chained him to a rock and sent an eagle to eat his liver was mild punishment compared to the curse laid on me.

It was just before I got past the creek north of the house that I realized my breath was reeking of that dreadful concoction from the jug, so I did the only thing I knew to do, since Daddy would kill me if he knew I'd been drinking: I plucked a handful of pine needles and chewed them up, spat half of them out, and swallowed the rest.

The needles killed the liquor breath, but I felt so terrible that I figured my face was probably taking on some of their color. When Daddy met me at the back door, he said, "My God, son, you look like hell, and you smell like a bottle of Pine Sol. What have you been eatin'?"

"Pine needles," I told him.

"Well, no wonder you look like that. Your momma saved you some biscuits and squirrel and gravy. They ought to taste better than pine needles. Next time, you take somethin' fit to eat when you camp out—Vieener Sausages or sardines or a chunk of fatback and cheese. Now you get in here and eat your braffus and get y'self cleaned up and get ready for church."

I managed to get down a biscuit and a squirrel hindquarter without throwing up, and then I dressed for church. It was the longest service in my memory, with visions of hell every way I looked, and I swear the preacher's eyes caught mine every time I glanced his way. And, oh, those little burps of that witch's broth and pine needles. . . .

It would be many years before I touched liquor again after that wild night on the river, and I gave up pine needles for good.

After a few beers at Fort Jackson, I didn't drink again until a year or so into my first marriage. Jackie's folks were churchgoing teetotalers, like Mother, and not one of them would allow a drop of even the weakest of wines in the house. Daddy always did his drinking outside. He kept little fifths of whiskey hidden all over his shop and in the trunk of the car. I don't know what he chewed to kill the smell, but so far as I know, Mother never caught him at it. If she had, he would have simply exploded and declared that it was his house and he could bring any damned thing into it that he wanted to. I guess he thought it wasn't worth the trouble.

Sometime during the second year of marriage to Jackie, I was introduced to vodka. I mean, there was some vodka in that communal jug, but it had lost all its personality in the crowd.

The ironic thing is that the person who introduced me to it was none other than the brother of my wife, who had a very negative opinion of alcohol and would not so much as sip wine. She definitely wouldn't allow booze in the house, which had been fine with me because I didn't drink. Shit, in those days I didn't even swear. But thangs, as they say, change.

Now one night her brother and I were cruising down Highway 69, south out of Columbus, when he told me to pull over on the shoulder. We stopped at the edge of some woods, maybe a mile from his folks' house. He motioned to the exact spot where he wanted me to stop.

"Come on," he whispered.

I had no idea what he was up to, but since he was into church and known to be a *good boy,* I assumed that we were not on a dark mission of any sort—you know, after *sheep.*

He stood looking at the woods in the moonlight, then decided he knew which way to go. I followed him a few feet into the trees, where he pointed to a log, barely recognizable as such to me, but he knew. He bent over and fished something out from behind it and held it up to me.

"Know what this is?"

I couldn't make out much, but it looked like a flat bottle.

"Looks like a whiskey bottle."

I heard him twist off a cap, and then he lifted the bottle and chugged something from it. He whistled softly, breathlessly.

When he got his breath back, he said, "It's *vodka,* and it's strong stuff." He held it out to me. "Take a slug."

I took the bottle and stood there a few seconds wondering just what the hell was going on, then shrugged, tilted it back, and swallowed long and deep.

Now *I* was the one struggling for air. Oh, Lord, it was liquid fire shooting down my gullet, gathering into a hot ball in my stomach, then radiating out into my capillaries.

"Oh, my Lord," I finally managed. "My sweet *Lord!*"

"It's fine, ain't it?"

I drew a deep breath and said, "Yeah, but it shonuff burns, don't it?"

"Shonuff good too."

"Man, Jimmy, that stuff works fast. I can feel it in my fingers and toes."

"I can feel it *everywhere.*" He took another slug from the bottle and handed it back to me.

Another chug, another shot of esophageal fire right into my stomach. I was buzzing like a June bug against a screen door, trying to get to the light.

"That's all for tonight." He leaned down and put the bottle back. "Gotta save some for another time."

While we were walking back to the car, he said, "The good thing about vodka is that it don't leave much smell on your breath. Chew a little gum and nobody can tell."

"Yeah, that's good, that's good." I sure as hell didn't want to eat another handful of pine needles.

Oh, man, that felt *awfully* good. Just enough to generate a nice buzz, but no vile taste in the mouth, no stomach churning, no sense of guilt. I dropped him off at the house and drove home, doing the vodka cruise.

So my appreciation for that particular kind of liquor began that night in the woods on Highway 69. If her brother could hide vodka and drink it, then so could I. I started stashing the stuff in ammunition cans in a closet, and I'd slip a drink whenever I thought I could do it without being suspected. She never caught me.

Actually I drank very little until along toward the end of that marriage. When things started falling apart, I would from time to time get smashed, but I was always a fairly pleasant drunk.

The only long, drawn-out binge occurred during the summer of 1971, when I made my third trip to Europe. The first two were study trips, during which I attended Southampton in southern England during the summers of 1969 and 1970. On campus I took postgrad courses in English literature, history, architecture, and art, and then our professors went with us on a cruise to the Mediterranean. There we learned—hands-on, as it were—the history, geography, and architecture of Portugal, France, Spain, Italy, Greece, Yugoslavia, and Bulgaria.

The problem with those tours was that they were precisely that: tours. I got tired of learning about dead people and places and times—I wanted to experience Europe and its people apart from the madding crowd. I wanted to dig in with my bare hands and feet and savor all it had to offer. And I wanted to drink whenever the urge arose, not when some tour guide or professor dictated the time and place.

In June of 1971 three other guys and I flew to London, rented a VW bus, traveled up and down Great Britain, ventured up to Scotland, and looped back down through Wales.

I got heavy into the booze only a couple of times before we left for Paris. On one binge I ended up in a nurses' training school dorm in London, where I shared a narrow bed with a former Playboy Club bunny. She would sneak me to the bathroom, bring food to the room, and keep me supplied with liquor, mostly cherry brandy, which she apparently had a big stash of. I don't remember how many nights I stayed there. Maybe two. I was drunk most of the time, but surprisingly well-behaved, as one tends to be when he knows that making noise might result in a few days in a London jail. I did pee out the window one night but only once: damned if I didn't hit someone two stories below.

A voice boomed up, "Who frowed piss down here. You lazy bitch! Go to the *WC!* All over me goddamn *wash!*" There was a lot more yelling, but I had closed the window and retreated to the safety of our bed. The golden shower could have come only from one of two rooms, so I figured we were dead. I woke the girl up and discussed the matter with her. She just laughed.

In a few minutes there was a knock at the door.

"Oh, Lord, now it's not funny," she whispered. "What are we going to do? They're going to know it came from this room or the one below."

"Tell'm it could have come from the roof."

"What?"

"The roof. Somebody coulda thrown piss off the roof."

"Dear God," she muttered, "you crazy-ass Americans!"

She spoke in hushed tones with somebody for a few seconds, then returned to bed.

"What'd they say?"

She was giggling like a child.

"You pissed on one of the head nurses while she was stringing out clothes to dry. She thought some girl had peed in a can or jar and poured it out the window. God, she's mad."

"What did you tell her?"

"What you told me to tell her."

"You mean—"

"I told her that someone could have thrown urine off the roof.

"Wasn't urine—it was mine."

She didn't think that was funny, but she started laughing again anyway. "She said . . . she said. . . ." She was stifling the giggles. "She asked, 'Now why would somebody "frowe" piss off the roof of a three-story building in the middle of the night? That's the kind of thing *lads* do!' And I told her that I didn't know, but that it didn't come from *this* room."

"Well, I guess you kept me out of jail again."

"What are the chances? What are the damned chances of whizzing out a window at night and hitting someone?" Then she broke up again.

"Here's a question for you: Why would a head nurse use words like *frowe* and *piss?* That sounded like someone from the East End."

"She *is* from the East End. I guess that when someone pisses on you and your laundry, you revert."

I reached down and took a long slug of brandy, and then she took a draw.

"Promise me you won't whiz out the window again."

"You got it, you got it. It'll be tough, but I'll try the bottle."

After we flew to Paris, the drinking began in earnest. I had already asked for a divorce, and I had decided to let my high-school contract expire, leaving me without a job for the first time since I was fifteen. It was time to flush my head of the old world and prepare it for the new, whatever the nature of it might be.

And flush it I did, every chance I got.

In Piran, Yugoslavia, I managed to find myself in competition with the town's vodka-drinking champ, whom I drank under the table one afternoon, largely because he had been drinking all day up to the point of the challenge. Midnight Cowboy they called me.

I was so rowdy that night that my friends locked me in a room on the third floor of the building we were staying in. They took my clothes, leaving me nothing but my cowboy hat. They forgot about the drain pipe that ran past a window to the street—and I discovered it. In no time at all I was snatching up and hurling steel garbage cans down the brick street out front, which our hosts, a couple of Yugoslavian sailors we'd picked up on the way, feared might run afoul of the local police department's sense of propriety, no matter its therapy for me. (In those days Yugoslavia was still a communist country, and their police were essentially military units armed with submachine guns.) The guys snatched me up and lugged me upstairs again, poured some more vodka in me, and stashed me in a bathtub after I passed out, wrapping the whole thing with fish net secured with rope to be certain that I behaved myself the rest of the night.

I spent much of an afternoon in Munich slugging beer in a beer hall and spreading the gospel of the South. I stood on tables and sang "Dixie" and gave the rebel yell until I was hoarse. The Germans ate it up.

On the way back to our VW bus, I passed out and fell back onto the hood of an MG owned by a German thug who apparently didn't want a drunk American as an ornament. He came out of a bar, snatched me off the car, and started beating the ever-lovin' hell out of me as my friends just stood and watched, held at bay by his buddy's clearly visible holstered pistol hanging beneath an armpit.

My body took a pretty good hammering, but I didn't know anything about it until the next day, when I woke up in an abandoned barn with blood on my pillow. According to all reports, I just sat and lay on the ground while the punk took target practice with his fists and feet.

Revenge was on my mind then. I drove into Munich and picked up a quart of sulfuric acid at an apothecary, ostensibly to clean some stones I had found, and I set out with my buddies to find that MG. After dark I planned to melt down everything on it that wasn't fiberglass, rubber, or glass. I did not drink a drop all afternoon.

We patrolled the streets without success on into the early evening, right on up until a drunk German mathematics professor turned illegally in front of me and I plowed into him. It wasn't much of an accident, but I spent the rest of the night in a Munich police substation trying to get it all sorted out. Luckily he lit up the test strip when the police arrived at the scene of the collision, so I ended up in the clear. What was weird to me was that in that police station, right next to the soft-drink dispenser, stood a machine loaded with beer. Go figger. . . .

Somehow I survived that summer and came home prepared to open the door to the rest of my life.

I have been a reasonable drinker over the years, and generally my experiences with the hard stuff were pleasant enough, but I do recall a few occasions when I wished I had been a teetotaler.

I was off on a tour in Montana one time when, at a reception following my reading at Carroll College in Helena, the host, a young assistant professor, offered me a choice of drinks. I looked around his modest quarters, troubled that he had drawn the short straw. Typical grad-school decor—Early American Ghetto.

"Whatcha got?"

He pointed to two massive jugs on the kitchen counter—looked like they'd come off an Ozarka truck. I was reminded of a cartoon I saw in the *New Yorker* once. A big eighteen-wheel tanker was tooling along on a highway, and on its side was printed CHEAP WHITE WINE.

"Your choice of wine, red or white. Or I could mix you something." He seemed so anxious to please.

"Tell you what," I said. "I'm not much in the mood for wine, so just mix me something."

"What about a Manhattan? I make a mean Manhattan."

"Manhattan's fine. That'll do nicely." I remembered fondly George Garrett's Manhattans.

I began mingling with the small group then, and my host brought me my drink, which was indeed mean. It was everything that mean can mean: bad, gross, wretched, execrable, crummy, yucky, foul, fetid, corrupt, septic, heinous, onerous; it was, in short, *most* unpleasant. But I couldn't tell him that. George would have sipped it all evening without so much as a grimace.

I methodically dipped my upper lip into it until I could work my way to the kitchen sink, where I jettisoned it. It took two hot peppers to kill the taste. I tried a long time to sort out between my mind and tongue precisely what he had put in it to render it so unpalatable.

But it wasn't by any means the worst drink I've ever had. No. Bad as it was, it in no way approaches the villainous nature of a drink that Lilla Mae Gray Marshall, who retired from the SHSU English Department a few years back, served me once.

At the time of this memorable drink I was working every kind of odd job I could pick up, just to get by. My second wife, Sharon, and I were funneling all our resources into that money-trap house of ours up on the ridge, and my university salary, plus what I earned teaching extension courses in the prison system for Lee College, just wouldn't stretch far enough. I kept up a couple of trailer parks and did wiring and plumbing for Ruth Turner, rebuilt a diesel tractor engine for her; mowed an industrial park for Gibbs Brothers; did wiring for Ed and Genevieve Sandhop; built a fence for Patsy Copeland; with Donald Coers's help wallpapered Eleanor Mitchell's house; spray painted Coer's old VW Beetle; completely renovated Don Stalling's house one summer and added a carport; built a porch for Jack Kerr that, contrary to his claims, never leaked; put a roof on Ms. Felder's garage on 19th; completely resodded Kent Jones's and Sarah Adell Hall's lawns; did landscaping, mechanical, carpentry, electrical, and plumbing work for dozens of other people in Huntsville; refinished floors and painted houses and hung ceiling fans and sold fruit trees that Sharon and I grew from seeds and budded or grafted one little tree at a time. Sharon, in addition to serving as my co-worker on many of those jobs, refinished other people's antiques in our shop.

Well, this particular day I was doing some wiring for Lilla Mae—putting in receptacles, installing a ceiling fan, just odds and ends—and the toughest part was crawling around in her attic drilling holes and dropping wires. Of course it was the dead of summer. It always is when you're required to be in an attic for any length of time. (Every bloody time people want you to work in the attic, it'll be July, August, or September.)

I'd spent a good part of the afternoon wedged back between the rafters and joists, doubled over with a brace-and-bit (which will give you an idea of precisely how poor we were at the time), just enough room to turn the damned thing, only a tiny flashlight to help me see what I was doing, but I wanted to finish the job so that I wouldn't have to go back up there. It was time for the last splice. Now, I thought Lilla Mae had turned all the power off—I told her to and I heard her flip the breakers and she yelled up that she had—but the leg I was working on still had juice in it (sounds like a big meal underway, don't it?), and when I cut the hot wire, I got jolted through the broken insulation on my pliers. I had a heavy sheen of perspiration, so, as they say in the trade, I got bit good.

I had been up there for hours, so that was it for me for the day. I taped the end of the wire I'd cut—right then I didn't care if it fed the freezer or Lilla Mae's great-aunt's iron lung in the back bedroom—and, still tingling, crawled down out of that attic, sweating like a Lister bag, battered with fiberglass insulation: looked like a cross between the Pink Panther and Straw Man, if you can imagine that particular coupling. Hot as the hinges of hell and still vibrating from that jolt of electricity, I was just generally disgusted with the world.

When Sharon and Lilla Mae walked out onto the lawn where I was standing, Lilla Mae asked pleasantly whether I might like a drink. I will not tell you what I said, because I frankly don't remember. Couldn't have been very civil. It might have started something like: "Does a frog have a watertight asshole?" Whatever, I made my point clear. *Yes, I wanted a drink.*

Well, bless Lilla Mae's heart, she offered water first, then a Diet Pepsi, finally iced tea, but I kept waving her off. "No, no, Lilla Mae. I do not want to quench my *thirst*—I want to quench my *memory*."

"Lilla Mae," Sharon said, "I think he means the hard stuff."

"At's right, Momma. Make it tall and strong."

I hosed myself down while she was mixing my drink. When I curled the hose back up, I looked at the puddle where I had been standing—you'd have thought a big pink panther had lost a major battle there.

Lilla Mae came up behind me. "Well," she said, "I didn't have much variety, but I did the best I could. Careful, though, it's probably pretty potent." She handed me what looked like a rum and coke in a big tea glass. Full, right to the rim, maybe thirty-six ounces, maybe forty. *Yes!*

"Oh, Lilla Mae, it'll be all right. I'll bet I've had worse." I held my breath and sipped off the top, then tilted the glass back and took a deep draw.

Unh-unh. I had not had worse. Not to that point in my life. Not since.

You know that Willie Nelson song that has a line that goes "Their breath was hard as kerosene"? Well, I knew right then and there what those old boys had been drinking.

"How is it?" Lilla Mae asked.

She swam before my eyes like someone in clear, deep water. "*What* is it?"

"The only thing I could come up with. Scotch and Diet Pepsi. I doctored it up a little, though, like a Bloody Mary." She turned around to walk back to join Sharon in one of the flower beds, then said over her shoulder, "Let me know when you're ready for another."

I cannot fully describe the taste. Somewhere between aviation fuel and maybe WD-40 and. . . . No. Traces of salt, pepper, onions, lemon juice. Hell, I don't know. Words fail me. It was worse than any purgative you'd give a child or solution you'd rub on a horse. You'll just have to try one for yourself, whatever you'd call it. I wouldn't suggest you go to your local bar—or any bar anywhere, for that matter—and ask for that combination. "Hey, y'all," the bartender'd say, "listen what this fool has ast for. That'll brang on spontaneous combustion, boy, eat thoo glass and stainless steel. Not in my bar, you ain't gettin' nuthin' like that. Be pro-ject-ile vomitin' and die-rear all over the place. Now, tequila and Irish Spring handsoap I'll do. Maybe vodka and Scope. Do a little multicultural shit for you. But not nothin' like that. Not in my bar. My li-bility insurance don't go that far."

Well, when I finished that still-unnamed and indescribable concoction, holding my breath and slugging—I was after *oblivion*—I wiped my hand across my mouth and tried to assess my state while the drink was seeping into remote capillaries. I'd washed off most of the loose fiberglass, but, even with that anesthesia taking hold, I could feel it all down my back, in my shoes, in my shorts. I finally realized the effect of the drink on my empty stomach when I looked over at Lilla Mae and Sharon, who were floating in a distant flowerbed.

The four of them swam up to me and two asked whether I wanted another drink. I held the empty glasses out to the Lilla Maes and said no, I guessed what I really wanted was to get in my truck with Sharon and go on home. A terminally ill man prefers to die at home in the arms of his wife.

I remember little of the jerking, snorting trip—Sharon drove the old manual-transmission Ford the best she could. I immediately took to my bed and entered a world of uneasy dreams where pink panthers floated across a lawn upon which twin witches stirred a roiling pot, muttering, "Bubble, bubble, toil and trouble, Scotch and Pepsi, make it double, add some salt and add some pepper, stand aside and watch him *fester.*" I did not touch alcohol for a very long time, almost a week.

Then there was the Heaven Hill hell that I suffered one afternoon when I had my little cattle operation outside Huntsville.

I generally kept a bottle of whiskey hidden in the hay bales in the barn—you know, for medicinal reasons, as they say, snakebites and stuff like that—and this particular day I was so disgusted with the ongoing drought we were suffering through that I sought to ease the pain with a few slugs from the half-gallon jug of the cheapest booze I could lay my hands on, Heaven Hill. This was, after all, emergency whiskey, and its purpose was a long way from pleasing the palate or impressing anyone who might just happen to be watching when I broke it out.

It was the summer of 1980, I believe, and for days on end I had ridden my motorcycle out there to pump water from the ponds so that my cattle would not wither away like the grass they were supposed to be grazing on. The creek bed was deep dust, and I was feeding hay in late July—no rain for months. Nothing.

Every afternoon the storms would build, flatten on top, and darken into great bears roaring across summer, dormancy over, the rumble of appetite everywhere. Then they would rear and grumble, waving their windy arms, and mutter off to other places, finally hanging in the distance like healing bruises, torn apart by their own deep energies and raining themselves to nothing a hell of a long way from where I stood each evening watching the ponds dry up. I swore to my wife that I could see the dorsal fins of catfish feeding along the bottom.

Then one afternoon it just got to me. After feeding and watering the cows, I was leaning against an oak tree that stood at the end of the garden I had given up on weeks before, letting everything go. The cows came before the garden, and there wasn't enough water for both.

At some point I walked into the barn and fished out my Heaven Hill, took some ice cubes from the little freezer atop the refrigerator, filled a Dixie cup, then covered them with whiskey. I didn't even let it chill: threw it back and slugged it in one breath. Did it again. And again.

When the ice was gone, I turned the bottle up and chugged directly from it, for a while chasing it with water from a bottle in the refrigerator, then taking it straight.

I had had nothing to eat since lunch, so that whiskey hopped on my Capillary Express and rode all over me in a matter of less than five minutes, I would say, though I sure as hell wasn't timing it.

Blistering hot, I yanked off my T-shirt and jumped into the nearest pond with just my shorts on, floundered around awhile with the annoyed cows looking on, then clawed up the muddy bank and got back on my bottle.

At some point, overcome by the inner and outer heat, I passed out near the end of the garden and lay there comatose for an hour or so, long enough for the sun to lose itself in the trees along the creek.

And what I woke up to was a misery so great, a pain so intense, that a number-three washtub of Heaven Hill wouldn't have made me forget it, unless I drowned myself in it.

"Holy shit! What the hell *is* it?"

My arms and legs, belly and chest, were blistered, and my back was on fire.

I lunged toward the pond and dove headfirst into the muddy slime, rolling over and over until the burning subsided enough that I could at least *see.* I had been in such pain that I ran blind into that pond.

When I finally managed to get back up to the spot where I had been lying, I could see where I had wallowed during my whiskey-laden sleep, and what I had been rolling in was a thick patch of bull nettle, dry as everything else but still packing one hell of a punch.

I was trying to find my shirt when I heard a horn at the gate. Since it was late, well past time for me to be home, Sharon had driven out to check on me.

"Mawright!" I yelled. "Mawright. Go on home. Be there dreckly."

But she would have none of that. I was stumbling drunk, couldn't find my keys, couldn't find my shirt. I *did* see the Heaven Hill bottle, which I kicked toward the pond.

"Come on, Paul. Get in the car. You're going home with me. You're in no condition to ride that motorcycle."

I felt for my keys and shirt again, didn't find them.

"Arright, arright. I'm comin'."

She yelled back: "You locked the gate behind you, and I don't have a key. Do you have a key?"

"Yeah, got keeeeeee." I slapped my shorts pockets again. "Ownknow where the key is."

I walked up to the gate and tried to climb over it, slipped and fell twice.

"Can you get through the wire?"

"Sher, sher. I can squeeze through."

I slid one foot and leg between two strands of barbed wire and had just started slipping the rest of me through when my inner left thigh touched the hot wire I had strung to keep calves from getting out of the pasture.

Now, I had been tingling for hours, but that was nothing like what I felt trapped between those wires. I was still coated with wet mud from the pond and dripping with sweat and my shorts were soaked, so I was literally wrapped in electricity, *cocooned.*

Oh, it was sobering! I shrieked and flung myself away from the fence—luckily to the right side—and landed and rolled back on my ass, tumbled, and came to rest in a sitting position. I looked up at Sharon, who was just standing there in front of the car shaking her head.

"I don't even want to know," she said. "Just get in the car. The real world will come back tomorrow."

When I was settled in and belted, she looked over at me, almost naked and completely coated with mud.

"My God, you look like something out of *National Geographic.* You ought to be riding in the trunk."

And so ended my afternoon on Heaven Hill. I do not wish to go back.

Rats!

A few years back David Bottoms, who looks for all the world like an Oklahoma-peanut-farmer-turned-hippie, came out with a collection of poems titled *Shooting Rats at the Bibb County Dump.* Won the Walt Whitman Award with it. Published by Morrow. Nominated for a Pulitzer. Big-time stuff.

I was rereading *Shooting Rats* one day and ran across Dave's title poem, which describes how these good ol' boys, loaded on whiskey and beer, would go out to the Bibb County dump (on the Georgia poetry circuit, I believe) and shine their car lights out over the mounds of refuse and unlimber their rifles on the rats too dumb to keep their eyes closed. See, young rats'll stare with both eyes at a light every time; the older ones will use only one eye, and you don't know whether it's the right or left, so you can't decide what side to shoot on. You shoot and you either miss completely, maybe clip an ear, or you hit them right between the eyes, but you can never be sure. Clever they are, old rats. That's why they're old. The young ones are dumber than frogs. They'll stare at a light even on a moonlit night, while a frog won't—and there's another story.

Dave describes how rats react to a head or gut shot. Not pretty stuff. But if you're going to read a poem about shooting rats at the county dump, you're not in a mindset for aesthetics. Rats and garbage dumps, taken together or separately, generally don't make the Chamber of Commerce brochures. As a matter of fact, they seldom make poetry.

Well, what I'm getting around to here—and you're probably saying, "Finally, thank you, Jesus"—is my own rat shooting back in Mississippi when I was a boy. It was my earliest exposure to guns and hunting and high finance.

At age twelve I was a professional hunter.

I put that on a line by itself and italicized it to let the gravity of the message sink in.

When I was a boy we had rats. Lots and lots of rats. Big, burly, aggressive rats, the kind that could whip every cat in the neighborhood and most dogs and were known to eat calves and small children and sever power cables and gnaw through steel panels on a barn. Now, in the house the folks went high tech and dispatched them neatly enough with d-Con (probably on the way to being outlawed by now anyway if it hasn't been already, thanks to the EPA and animal-rights people). They'd put out these little jar lids of greenish pellets in the kitchen and closets, the pellets would disappear, and in a couple of weeks the *odors* of the house would announce to all who entered that something in the walls or attic was with some reluctance returning to the dust from whence it came.

That was fast-working, sure-fire poison in those days, so the rats (and mice) just didn't last in the house. D-Con in the chicken house, though, was another matter. And that's where we had the biggest problem: rats fattening on chicken feed. Sprinkle poison pellets out there, and you get dead chickens, not because chickens are too dumb to distinguish between their food and rat poison but because chickens are trusting. They never believe you'd give them anything that wasn't good to eat. This is a distinguishing difference between chickens and most children—along with the feet, feathers, beaks, and eyes set in the sides of the head.

We had a big, long chicken house with feed pans outside in the fenced-in yard. The chickens got cracked corn every day, and Mother would now and then toss in some ground-up oyster shells "for their *craw,*" a mysterious organ that apparently only chickens have (though I heard my mother say on many occasions that she had had a *crawful* of me). The chickens, a couple of dozen or so, would descend in a great flurry, cluck whatever grace they were required to say—I determined by their talking in strange tongues that most of them were Assembly of God, like us, with a couple of haughty hens that acted like Catholics and one heathen rooster—and contentedly take their meal.

But of course they never ate it all. And what they left, the rats scurried out to finish off. They would never venture into the yard while the chickens were feeding. This was something the chickens and rats worked out between themselves after a rooster hammered the ever-loving hell out of a rat at a feed pan one day—I saw it happen. It was no match. Beak, wings, and spurs went to work in a great whirlwind of feathers and dust like an apocalyptic scene from the Bible, and the rat found his hole just before he had to make a new one. *Hell hath no fury like a hungry rooster with a rat between him and his rations* (Confucius, *The Sung Sun,* 12 April, 490 B.C., sec. 1:3. I don't know how they figured out the B.C.).

When the chickens were gone, the rats would slip out of their holes and literally polish the pans and sweep the yard around them. People who think rats are nasty just haven't seen them clean up around feed pans in a chicken yard.

Now I had a .22 single-shot rifle that had been handed down from my grandfather to my father to me, and I was good with it. Once-varnished generic wood stock, once-blued metal, burnished by then to a sheen I could see my teeth in. I could head-shoot a squirrel at fifty yards every time, if I got a chance to draw a bead. If he was on the run, it might take three or four fumbling reloads, but I'd generally make him real sorry he'd gotten up that day before I took him home for Mother to batter (hell of a word, ain't it?) and fry up for breakfast or supper, head and all.

My father encouraged good shooting, because he liked squirrel meat and hated rats and because we were too poor for me to waste cartridges. The deal was that he would provide ammunition and pay me a nickel apiece for rats I head-shot, three cents for those that died a lingering death. A mouse brought a nickel wherever I shot him, since mice were much smaller and thereby more difficult targets, but mice were so low on the pecking order that they seldom showed up at the pans—mice don't mess with roosters *or* with rats, which is why they will be cleaning up the bones of the last rat *and* rooster *and* man. The mice'd wait around and come out at night after the rats had gone to bed and dine on whatever was left around the pans, generally in molecular measure, I'd say.

My stand was the ridge of the chicken house, where I'd take position while the chickens were eating. I hoisted my rifle onto the roof, climbed the fence, and stepped from a post top onto the slope, scrabbled with the rifle over rough shingles to the ridge, then straddled it, a leg and arm on either side. Rifle loaded and cocked, steady on the roof edge and trained on the feed pans below, I waited like a figurehead on the prow of a ship—the only way I would move was if the chicken house did, and this was not often.

The wait was short, intense. Just as the chickens cleared the pans, a gray head would fill one of the many holes that dotted the edge of the yard. I cradled the head in the rear sight, the fine post of the front sight weaving from cheek to cheek, while the little whiskers and ears twitched, testing the air. I dared not fire then—I had to let him get away from the hole. I'd lost too many to a reflex retreat.

In time he'd make his move to one of the feed pans and busy himself with the paltry leavings. The thin crack of a .22 short, and I almost always had my rat. One rat per stalk (slightly less than corn) was a typical yield, though sometimes they were hungry enough to ignore the noise of the rifle and the silence and stillness of a dead comrade and rush the feed pans. Oh for a repeating rifle! Once I had five stretched out lifeless in the yard before I left my post—a full quarter, but for one neck shot.

So it was that at age twelve I rose to the status of professional hunter. No one snapped pictures of me kneeling before my kills, no menacing heads with cold glass eyes hung over my bed, no writer from *Outdoor Life* or *Field & Stream* came calling. But I knew what I was, and I was proud. Arms and legs scratched and dimpled by the sandy shingles, I would gather my rats and carry them triumphantly to the back door and present them on the steps, then carefully clean my rifle and wait for my father to examine for head shots and pay me off. But for place and time, religious taboo, and my mother's fury, it would have been a moment for a beer and cigar for the hunter home from the ridge.

The only time I can recall that I actually had fun with a rat occurred when I hatched a plan to avenge the death of my dog, Lady.

A little background: We were hunting on, or near, the old home place south of Millport, Alabama—my brother, five years younger, my father, and I—and there had been an early freeze or two and the leaves were well off, making still-hunting for squirrels difficult, especially with the dead, dry leaves underfoot. So we had brought Lady, my mixed-breed dog—overweight and probably as old as I was—to track and tree the squirrels. She had been reliable over the years in this role, and I always loved having her along anyway. She loved being with us. Our other two dogs were strictly coon dogs and wouldn't waste their time on a squirrel.

It was a fiercely hot day, as October days can be in the Deep South, and we had stripped down to T-shirts (in Daddy's case, is was what today is called a "wife beater"), tying our jackets around our waists. Keeping up with Daddy was tough. He always knew where he wanted to go, and he covered as much territory as possible. Still-hunting the early part of the season was a slow, deliberate process in which stealth was everything, and you might move half a mile an entire morning. Hunting squirrels with a dog meant moving fast until the dog picked up a fresh trail, so you didn't care how much noise you made. Squirrels would typically hunker down in the last tree they had gone up, keeping the trunk or a limb between them and the threat on the ground. (This is why it is important to have at least two people along, so that they can stand on opposite sides of a tree and spot the squirrel. Three people make it even easier.)

If the heat was miserable for us, Lady was suffering worse. She was a big dog, white with brown spots, and heavy in her advancing years, so she was really in no mood to hunt squirrels. Daddy would shout for her to GET ON OUT THERE AND HUNT, and she would range out a few dozen feet in front of us, then come back to me, her tongue lolling, wanting her ears rubbed. He would give her a light kick on the rump—which I didn't like but didn't dare say anything—and she would lower her tail and trot out again into the woods before us, run her nose along the ground a little while, then come sidling back. A couple of times she yelped along a trail, then false-treed, which put Daddy into an even worse mood.

"Keep on, dog," he'd say; "just keep on messin' with me. You better get your fat ass out there and hunt. A dog that don't hunt ain't worth killin'."

Every time he said something like that, I'd get this chill down deep inside in spite of the outer heat. When he used that tone with me—"Arright, boy, you just keep on!"—it meant that sooner rather than later I'd hear his "Bible Belt" come out, *flapflapflapflap* through the loops, and he'd bear down on me, working that doubled belt from the back of my head to my heels, and no matter the wailing and begging, once that fury was let loose, it would not slack off until he'd worn his wrath out, like a savage thunderstorm rumbling and flashing and lashing until its fury is done.

"Lord," I kept saying to myself, "make her get on out there and hunt. I don't want him to beat her." I just didn't know how I'd take that, didn't know whether I could watch that awful belt of his flaying my dog, didn't know what I'd do.

"Go on, Lady," I whispered to her, "go hunt. Go hunt, Lady. Find a squirrel." But all she wanted was to lie down and rest and have her ears rubbed.

Then he came roaring over through the underbrush, his boots heavy in the leaves, and he kicked her to her feet and ordered her again to hunt, to GET OUT THERE AND HUNT! She rose, tail tucked, ears flattened, and trotted out maybe twenty feet and stopped, looked back toward me. My brother told me many years later that it was the first time he had heard Daddy use the word *fuck.*

I don't know what all he said. What I remember is his raising that shotgun and aiming it at her. Before I could say a word, make a move in her direction, he had fired three times into Lady, broadside, and she flopped over, a great spray of blood brightening the pale-brown and yellow October leaves.

I couldn't do a thing. I had to accept the fact that the power I was witnessing was beyond anything I could deal with. Henry and I fell in line behind him as he slashed out of the woods that day, leaving Lady just lying there for the buzzards, a pale lump speckled with blood. But what could I do? Through a blurry curtain of tears I saw him fish out three more shells and slide them into that Browning as he walked along. For what? There sure as hell wasn't anymore hunting to be done. I suspect it was to let me know that he wasn't beyond blowing me away if I said a word. I didn't. I don't know how long it was before I could talk to him again, but it was a very long time.

There is probably not a person alive who didn't from time to time plot revenge against one or both parents for some real or imaged injustice dealt him. After Daddy shot Lady, I desperately wanted him to suffer for his sin, but revenge against that man would have to be terminal or very subtle. I considered putting sand down the oil filler hole in his car or turning a cottonmouth loose under the driver's seat, but whether he actually convinced himself that I had done it or not, there was a chance he would think that I might have and take it out on me. Then I thought about putting rat poison in his food, but I wasn't sure I wanted him to *die* for killing Lady, especially since we needed his paltry paycheck from the Beneke toilet-seat factory to get by. I mean, if I could have been certain that he would just green up and vomit three or four days or have to live in the outhouse for a week with the screaming hot shits, I would have taken that route, but I just didn't know enough about rat poison to determine what dosage a human could stand without keeling over. They didn't put that kind of directions on the label. I would just have to wait and watch, be patient.

I began hunting squirrels at probably age ten, at first with that .22 single-shot rifle, then with a .410 shotgun. I preferred still hunting to hunting with a dog, because there were those long stretches of still silence during which I could fantasize about anything and everything, mostly girls. Before daylight I'd make my way down through the woods along the Luxapalila and find one of my favorite hunting spots and lean against a tree several yards away from a hickory with evidence of recent feeding beneath it and daydream until a breakfast-minded squirrel timbered across my vision. Then I'd pick him off and just let him lie there while I waited for more to come along. I usually got between two and five early in the season when the leaves were on and I wasn't so visible to them. Besides, it was a lot easier to stalk quietly before the leaves had fallen.

We always ate the squirrels that Daddy and I killed. Mother would fry them or make squirrel stew or squirrel and dumplings; sometimes she would fry them for breakfast, and we'd have them with squirrel gravy over biscuits. (Hey, don't knock it if you ain't tried it.)

Most weeks we brought in ten or twelve between us, enough for two or three meals, and everybody got plenty of squirrel. But if we had a lean week, or one of us didn't get to go hunting, we might have only one or two on hand. When that happened, Daddy got them. That was the gospel according to David: if there were only one or two squirrels cooked up, he got them, and that was that.

Now one thing Daddy really loved was squirrel brains. They were a delicacy to him and one of the grossest things to eat that I could imagine. So though I had to shoot chicken-pen rats through the head with my .22 to drop them on the spot and collect my nickel bounty, my instructions were to shoot a squirrel through the rib cage so that neither the front nor hindquarters nor head would be damaged. Once they were hit, they generally went nowhere but to the ground. If the bullet didn't kill them, the fall did.

Mother would fry the head up with the front and back quarters, and Daddy would pop open the skull with the handle of a kitchen knife, then scoop the little globs of brain out with a blade of his pocketknife. It was a ritual. If we had three or four squirrels, he would eat the brains of every one of them. My brother and I used to joke that if Daddy kept on eating that stuff, he would develop a craving for hickory nuts.

OK, it was in late November, three or four weeks after he shot Lady, the day before or after Thanksgiving because Daddy had to work and I didn't have to go to school, and I went squirrel hunting that morning. All the leaves were off, so I knew that anything I brought in I would have to kill right at dawn, since there was no way I could move with stealth through the woods. I nailed one little gray just as the sun was lighting up the top branches of the hickory I was watching. There wasn't a nut hanging, but hope springs eternal in squirrel brains, so this little guy was making certain that one hadn't been overlooked.

When I got home with him, I went into the kitchen and got a pan and knife and took the squirrel out into the backyard to skin and gut him and cut him up. The dogs always got what Mother wouldn't cook. I was skinning the squirrel in the sun behind the well house, where it was warm, when I glanced over into the chicken pen and saw a rat cleaning up after the chickens had eaten. When I got in from hunting, I had just leaned the .22 against the steps at the back door. I always did that, since I sat on the steps and cleaned my gun after every hunt—Mother wouldn't let me clean it inside. I laid the squirrel down and slipped around the well house and got my rifle, then eased over next to the well and drew a bead on the rat, who was too busy to pay attention to me.

It was a long shot, but I got him, though I caught him through the middle and he almost made it back to his hole before he collapsed. After I picked him up, I carried him back where the squirrel was and laid him alongside it. Almost precisely the same size. As a matter of fact, if I had taken the feet and tail off both of them, I'm not certain the average person would have been able to tell one from the other. The wheels were turning.

In short order I had the rat skinned, gutted, and quartered, and the dogs took care of the squirrel. As was the custom, I took him in and left the pan beside the sink, where Mother would wash him and get him ready to cook.

"Hey, Mother," I yelled into the living room, where she was doing something, "I didn't get but one this morning. He's by the sink."

"Well, your daddy's gon' get it without you want me to freeze him for later, unthaw him when we get some more." (She always said *unthaw.*)

"That's OK. He can have him."

So it was that that evening Mother fried chicken and the rat (in that order, thank God), which, true to form, Daddy demanded. He got all four quarters and the head. I could barely contain myself while I worked my way through a thigh and drumstick and creamed potatoes and all.

When he was through with his chicken and had cleaned the rat leg bones, he picked up the head and struck it a quick blow with the handle of his table knife, then ceremoniously removed his pocketknife and opened the small blade, flicked the little pieces of skull off onto his plate, and scooped out the brains.

"Not much meat on this'n, but lots of brains," he said when he had finished. Then he wiped the pocketknife off with his napkin and put it up and leaned back in his chair and looked at me.

"Man, them thangs is good. Maybe next time you'll hunt better and brang in enough squirrel for everbody."

I was fairly choking but managing to keep myself under control. "Yessir, I'll try harder."

Then, oh then, he said to Mother, "Hey Zeke." (That was his name for her, shortened from Zealon, a name I have never heard appended before to anything or anybody.)

Mother looked over at him.

"We got any of that yeller cheese in the house?"

That was it. I was still chewing whatever I had last put in my mouth, and I simply lost it. I spewed food all across the table, even splotched my brother, then stumbled for the door.

Blinded by tears—not of grief or rage this time but uncontrollable mirth—I managed to get out and down the steps, and I fell to my knees in the yard and laughed until I got it out of my system, and that took a while. The three of them were leaning out the door looking down, wondering what the hell was wrong with me. I figured I was in for a whipping, but that was OK too: I had gotten my revenge.

Once I left Sand Road and the lucrative world of killing rats, I thought that I was done with them. By the time I moved out, the chicken house was gone anyway, my parents having come slowly to the realization that buying store-bought eggs and chickens already plucked, cut up, and packaged made more sense than spending all that money and time fooling around with a herd of hens and fattening a den of rats. I don't know who won, me or the rats, but I saw no more of them when the chickens were gone.

I had a few brief battles with one or two many years ago when they got in my shop in Huntsville and broke into two boxes of Christmas wreaths and ate anything that might pass as items on a rat menu. I tried my damnedest to shoot one with a .22, but I never could get a shot, so I took them out with rat traps baited with cheese or pecans.

Alas the war is on again. I walked into my university office a few weeks ago and found popcorn kernels scattered all over the floor and desk and shelves, the little germ missing from the tip of every kernel. But the critter was into bartering and left me several nice little droppings in payment for the popcorn.

A couple of evenings later, I had a night class on editing and publishing, so the students were working in the Texas Review Press office, which adjoins mine. I heard one of them say, "There's something up there making noise." When I looked out of my office, she was pointing to the ceiling, where indeed something was making enough noise that you'd figure they were getting ready for some serious housekeeping.

"More than one," I said, and then I told the students about what happened to my popcorn stash and detailed the collection of rat turds I had accumulated.

"Judging by my ballistics test, one of those rats is *huge.*" I pointed to the ceiling. "That was probably him moving in a couch."

"Ewwww. . . ." "Gross!" "Nasty things." Etc.

As I drove home that night, I tried to figure out how best to go about doing battle with the gray ghosts. The .22 was out, since the UPD would likely frown on my firing even rat shot in my office. And my grand little surefire rat killer was out, since it would make a hell of a lot more noise than the rifle.

See, I bought from Dixie Arms this little brass device with a hammer and a short barrel that has a primer-cap nipple on it, just like on a musket. There's a trip lever right at the end of barrel with a bait pan cast into it. You load the barrel with a charge of black powder, pack it tightly with aluminum-foil wadding, place a primer cap on the nipple, put some sort of irresistible bait in the pan, cock the thing by wedging in the sear, and place it in a likely spot for rats. When the critter touches the bait and puts the least little pressure on the pan, the sear trips; the hammer flies home; the cap sprays fire into the powder charge; and that ball of aluminum foil sends the rat straight to Ratdom Come (kinda like Kingdom Come, only this place is just for rats). Lots of smoke and noise, though, which I assume the UPD would not be entertained by.

So I decided to do the proper thing and report the interloper to the authorities on campus, who in a couple of days sent over a solution: three little rectangular pieces of thin cardboard (maybe 7 by 3½ inches) coated with some truly strong sticky stuff that is supposed to keep the rat at the trough much longer than he intended to stay. (Kinda like flypaper, only for rats.) No directions whatsoever. Had to be their answer for a rat trap, though, so I dutifully peeled off the protective paper, set one down by one of my file cabinets, and laid a Ritz Cracker at the end of it.

The next day the cracker was gone, but there was no indication that the pad had been touched. So I rearranged things: I laid a Ritz right in the middle of the piece of paper. I'd already wondered about what would happen if the rat got just one or two feet stuck and decided to take off, dragging the cardboard along with him, so I set a half cement block (which I use for bookends) across one corner of it. If he was big enough to move that block, I'd bring in a shotgun loaded with buckshot. It would clearly be a case of self-defense, so what could the UPD say?

Next morning the Ritz was gone, but the only evidence that the rat had been there was a light coating of fur on the paper, as if he had eaten the cracker and taken a nap. I slumped in my chair and wondered just what to do.

When I got back to Willis, I ran by D & M Hardware. Mr. Lee, the owner, would have the answer. And he did, in the form of one of those old-fashioned wooden rat traps with a spring-loaded steel loop designed to crush the biggest rat's skull when he grabs the bait.

I baited it up the next day with a ball of savory cheese and waited.

For a couple of days the trap sat unsprung in my office, the ball of cheese untouched.

Sez I, "Must be a squirrel. No rat could resist Velveeta."

The third morning I opened the office door and saw, brethren and sistren, one *huge* rat lying there with a big grin on his face, the steel loop right across his head and in deep. He didn't even get a nibble before boarding that freight to Ratdom Come.

Well, I reset the trap and waited, and several days later I caught the female, a bit smaller and, judging from her nipples, fully charged with ratlings.

That had to be it, I figured, though I left the trap there, baited and cocked, ready for any more of the tribe that might still be hanging around. I figured I'd broken some kind of rule, but I researched the issue thoroughly and found no mention of rat traps on the campus list of prohibited items. And as far as the American Rat Lovers Association went, they could go kiss one.

Nope, the story's not over. Not quite. As Yogi once said, "It ain't over till the fat lady farts," or something like that.

For years I have had a bobcat (*Felis rufus,* Latin for *Happy Ruffin*) standing on my rolltop desk in the office. Probably twenty pounds on the paw, he came to me by a circuitous route from former SHSU president Bob Marks, who judged that the animal was too pretty to leave on an East Texas roadside for buzzards to feast on and hauled him in for stuffing.

Bob the cat is a magnificent creature, and I have used him as a backdrop for quite a few photographs. Mounted on a big pine slab, he is in battle mode, his face up and turned to the right, fangs in full launch, and—if you let yourself imagine it—he is snarling. Below him is an old oil painting of Jesus, and you just know that the cat is there to protect him. The pity is that Jesus did not protect Bob.

OK, I'm getting to it. Be patient.

I got word the other day that there just might be a little money in the college budget for some shelves for one of the press storage rooms, so I turned around from my computer, which sits on a more modern desk, and reached for my steel measuring tape in one of the pigeon holes in my rolltop.

"Whoa, whuzzup here, Jesus?"

There were clumps of fur scattered over the top of the desk and cascading down onto Jesus's face.

"From where do this hair come from, mon frère?" I axed myself.

And then I looked up at pore old Bob, whose short, fluffy tail was nothing but a stem, like a rat's tail.

"What the hell. . .?"

And then I noticed that his upper lip had been completely gnawed away, and tufts were missing from the tops of his feet.

HE HAD BEEN IN A BAD FIGHT AND LOST!

Something had ripped him ass-under. (This is the way the evangelists used to put it when they cast out demons: they cast them *ass-under.* Or that's the way I heard it.) Ruined my bobcat is whut. Had to have been those rats!

"WHY?" I yelled at no one in particular. "Why the bloody hell would rats gnaw on a bobcat?"

I looked at Jesus for an answer, but he said nothing. Had to be a sign of the end times, the second coming maybe. Or global warming was at it again. It seems that everything is out of kilter in this old world.

Then it came to me: to build a nice, comfortable nest for the little darlings that Momma Rat must have been carrying.

Fancy this, now: those rats crawled up on my desk and attacked a creature that would have swallowed them whole had he been alive. I mean, they were gnawing off the upper lip and probably bracing their feet on Bob's big pearlies and ripping out tufts of hair a quarter of an inch from his claws.

I almost felt sorry for killing such fearless critters. When I stood back and surveyed the whole sweep of carnage in my office, though, I started wishing that I had made them suffer a bit longer.

"What I wish," I told some of my students after they had marveled at the desecration, "is that I had a LIVE bobcat that I could train to stand as still as stone on that board, heartbeat slowed to an occasional thump, and relish the speed with which a curious rat would disappear."

But I don't. All I have is a stuffed bobcat that looks like whatever brought him down gave him a real thrashing. Such a fine, fine animal he was.

So I apologize to both Bobs. I let y'all down. But hear this: I will keep a cheese-baited rat trap in that office as long as I stay there. I want to be ready if they ever invade again.

While I was sitting in the office one day looking up at my mangled bobcat, a notion came to mind. . . .

OK, I have this really fine little recorder—actually two, one that is mine and one that belongs to Texas Review Press—which I typically use in interviews, so I always have it handy. It occurred to me a couple of days before I caught the first rat that when they were pillaging my office, I might just leave it lying on the desk with the voice-activated setting on and perhaps pick up some of the noise that those interlopers had to have been making while they were rummaging through all my stuff and eating everything that wasn't sealed in glass or tin. My assumption was that they would not steal the recorder. Couldn't eat it, of course, but they might put it in a rathole sale.

So I reached over and flicked it on. Well—Glory be!—things worked out better than I had hoped. I discovered that I had recorded more than three hours of conversation between the male and female who'd staked out my office.

I transcribed the recording the best I could. Since I've never had a course in Ratease (or the broader-based Rodentese), I may not be precisely on target in a couple of places, but I think that I did a pretty good job with it. It took me quite a while to separate their chatter from all the clatter going on as they raided my popcorn stashes and rummaged around the office looking for anything edible; but my recorder downloads onto a computer, so I could slow things down, reduce background noise, enhance words, etc.

I have, of course, been selective, since I certainly don't have room to write down three hours of rat conversation. Besides, a lot of it was just prattle—maybe *rat*-tle is a better word.

So the pertinent bits of conversation begin. . . .

Male rat, I judged first by the depth of his voice: "Mojeen [which I took to be an abbreviated version of Imogene, but I might be wrong], ownknow when I have eat more popcorn. Two full boxes. The perfesser mus' really love that stuff."

"Umm-hmmmmm," came a female voice. "Got a bad thirst on, Roy. That stuff salty as . . . salt."

"Sho' glad we moved in here, Baby. I feel lak we wuz lucky to excape Russellville in one piece. Lak a third-worl' country down in there, I heard somebody say, 'cept I don't know what a third-worl' country is."

"I didn't thank they wuz but *one* worl', but what I know? Just a rat. Now, Roy, thangs wudn't so bad down there in Russellville. Plenty of places to stay. Lotsa cats to keep a eye out for is all."

"Been wondrin', Baby. . . . Quit rootin' around for a minute and lay down beside me. I need to axe you somethin'."

"Sho', Roy. Wuss on yer mind, Darlin'?"

"You seen them pitchers up there on the wall?"

"Unh-hunh, I seen'm. But I ain't studied'm or nuthin'. Why you axe?"

"Thas the perfesser with that skinny woman on that motorsickle, ain't it?"

Several seconds of silence. . . .

"Shonuff look lak him, don't it? Didn't know whut they wuz ridin', though."

"Mojeen, you know who I thank that is?"

"It's the perfesser, ain't it?"

"I know that, fool, but I thank he the one that live up in that great big ol' rock house on the hill, the one where Maudette and Earl and all their chirren wuz kilt. Shot two with a rifle and caught the res' in a big ol' trap."

"Roy, you thank thas the same guy?"

"I thank so. He might not still live up on the hill above Russellville, but I am purty sure it's him."

"Lord have mercy, Roy, we might done made a big mistake movin' into *this* guy's office. He be bad is whut. We done made a big mess, fersher, and I bet he mad as a ol' wet cat about it. Eat up all his popcorn too. He might get rough. We might could get hurt. We might could get *dead*."

"Mojeen, we lots smarter than Earl and Maudette and them chirren, smarter than that whole tribe. We OK. It's nice here. This gon' be our home from now on."

There was a long period of silence.

Then: "Roy. . . ."

"Yeah, Baby?"

Lots of rustling and grunting.

"Roy, them babies gon' be here purty soon, and we gon' have t'get ready for'm."

"We ready, Baby. Ain't we?"

"Naw, Roy. That place where we stay at ain't fit for no babies. I gotta have a nice nes'."

"What we gon' make a nes' out of? Ain't lak we can get leaves in here, or pine straw, or least it wouldn't be easy."

"Well, we gotta thank of sumthin."

"What about some of that stuff the perfesser call bubble wrap? It look lak it'd be sof'."

"I know that stuff you talkin' about, Roy. Be lak layin' down on balloons. Be cold too. We gon' need sumthin real sof' and warm for the chirren to lay on."

"Lak whut? Look around, woman. Ain't nuthin here to make no nes' out of, without we gon' tear up a bunch of paper."

"Look across there, Roy. See whut do you see."

"Where at? Look where at?"

"At *him.*"

"You talkin' about the guy in the pitcher?"

"Naw. *Above* that pitcher."

"You talkin' about that *bobcat?*"

"Yeah. Only it's *barb*cat."

"Whut you mean, *barb*cat?"

"Thas' the way you say it, ain't it? 'Member when Jackie Dee got tore up on that wahr down in Russellville? She tol' us it was *bob*wahr, but you said that it was *barb*wahr."

"At's whut it is, *barb*wahr. It's got barbs on it, little ol' sharp pieces of wahr stickin' out all over. They called *barbs* is whut."

"Then how come he ain't called a *barb*cat?"

"Because he ain't got barbs is why."

"Roy, you figger them teef and claws ain't barbs?"

"He be call a bobcat because his tail be bobbed off is whut."

"Hmmm. Well, I take y'word for it. But whut I wuz thankin' wuz how sof' his fur look. Make a mighty fine nes'. Thank about how good that would feel to me and the chirren."

"Mojeen, you talkin' about rippin' fur off a *bobcat!* You *crazy,* woman?"

"Roy, he dead. He ain't moved a inch long's we been here. Jus' lookin' off in the distance wif his mouf open lak he retarded."

"Well, it's a East Texas bobcat, ain't it? So he prolly is. [I was astonished at this perception.] I don't thank we ort to mess wif no bobcat, whether we thank he's dead or not or retarded or not."

"It is a *dead* barbcat, Roy. D-e-d. Or however them human beans spell it. *Dead.* He nailed down to a bode of some kind."

"I'm still real nervous about this, Mojeen. If he ain't, we jus' a snack to him."

"If he wudn't dead, Roy, we *would* be. He *dead,* Roy! And I am goin' to prove it."

"Mojeen, how you gon' prove that bobcat is dead?"

"Wif a meer."

"A meer?"

"Unh-hunh. You hold a meer in front of somebody's mouf and it will fawg over if they suckin' air."

"And perzackly where at we gon' get a meer from?"

"The perfesser's desk drawer is where at."

"He got meers in them drawers?"

"Shonuff. Two, to be perzack. One be a big ol' truck meer, and the other be a toof meer."

"Whut a truck meer is, Mojeen?"

"Go on a truck so's whoever drivin' it can see whut behind him. But it be *way* too big to lug up here."

"And whut a toof meer is?"

"So you can see y'teef to see if you got anythang stuck bertween'm."

"Lak whut?"

"Lak *anythang.* Strang. Hair. *Anythang.* Use y'magination, Roy." [Once again, I had no idea rats were so astute.]

"This is crazy is whut. So y'sayin' all we gots to do is drag out that toof meer and hold it in front of the bobcat's mouf and it'll fawg over if he alive?"

"Whut I'm sayin', yeah."

"Mojeen, this turnin' into somethin' not worf the trouble."

"You ain't speakin' for me, Roy, 'cause I got to thank about them chirrens that'll be here soon."

"Arright. Where the toof meer at? I go get it."

She must have pointed out the spot, because things got awfully quiet, except that I could hear something that sounded like one of my desk drawers being opened. Some grunting.

Then: "OK, Roy, thas it. Hol' it up here so's I can get a grip on it."

"Y'ont me to do it, Baby? That a man's job, seein' is a bobcat alive."

"Y'all ain't the onliest ones can handle thangs lak this." More grunting and fumbling about.

Then Mojeen giggled and said, "Hey, Roy, how come we know the toofbrush was invented in Arkansas?"

"Ownknow. How come?"

"Cause if it had of been invented anywheres else, they woulda called it a teefbrush."

"Lord, girl you a mess."

[Don't ask me about this. I don't know any more about rats than most other people, but I certainly have come to respect them more than I did.]

After a while Mojeen said, "Roy, ain't no fawg on the meer. He dead. That barbcat be dead as a rock."

"You sure, Baby?"

"Roy, wudn't no fawg, so I poked him in the eye wif the meer to make sure, and he didn't even *blink.* Ain't no live aminal gon' get poked in the eye wifout blinkin'."

"I rekkin."

"Come on up here and hep me get summa this fur."

For at least ten minutes all I could hear was the noise of the rats working my bobcat over. Then Roy's voice: "Lord have mercy, Mojeen, you know whut I done heard one time?"

"Whut?" The voice was muffled. I'm sure that her mouth was full of the fur of my bobcat.

"That a bobcat's upper lip is a afrodeeziak."

"Whut that mean?"

"Mean it give me more energy—you know, you know. . . ."

A long silence. Then: "Roy, I know whut that look mean. You don't need nuthin' to hep you out in that respeck."

More silence.

"Roy, get on away from that lip!" Silence. "Roy, get y'self away from that barbcat's lip. I done *tol'* you."

More silence.

"You crazy is whut, man. You had yo feet on that barbcat's *teef,* jes' gnawin' away at that lip. You sick is whut."

"Naw I ain't, Baby. You ort to try some of that lip. It shonuff good is whut."

"Get down from there right now, Roy, and hep me gather that fur."

I don't know what happened then, but I have my suspicions. After a few seconds I heard Mojeen squeal and then say, "Roy, not now, not here. We gots—Raw-*weeeeeeee.*"

As I say, I have a pretty good notion what went down, but that was the end of the recorded conversation.

So there you have it, folks: the only transcribed conversation of rats that I know anything about. After hearing them talk all that time, I felt really bad about killing them in the trap. But I keep finding things that make me glad that I did. Like holes in my V-8 cans—oh, yeah, they sucked up my vegetable juice. They bit right through that thin aluminum and washed down the popcorn. And if you think I'm kidding, I kept the cans as proof. Ate half a tube of Colgate toothpaste. I'm almost afraid to dig any deeper into the damage: I just know that eventually I'll wish I had killed them sooner.

The Bowhunter Asks for My Bladder

It was early January a few years ago out in West Texas, near Junction, just hours before whitetail season expired, and on a scaffold beside one of the cabins at Bob Winship's Rock Pile Ranch I had hanging a medium-size Sika buck I'd brought down with my rifle that morning; on the scaffold beside my Sika was a whitetail doe being skinned by a bowhunter.

I had just entered the serious phase of dressing the still-steaming carcass (they call it dressing, but what you're really doing is *undressing*), stripping out all the organs he wouldn't need anymore, when my bowhunter neighbor leaned over with his knife pointed across my shoulder at the Sika's entrails. I was a little uneasy.

"What're you gon' do with that bladder?"

I stopped hacking. I didn't know. Hadn't thought about it. What *can* you do with a deer bladder? You can't eat it, can you? I don't know that the most exotic restaurant in the world serves deer bladder. I can just hear myself saying to some prissy waiter poised with a delicate gold pen, "Hey, me'n the little lady here've decided on your Big Buck Bladder Platter, baked potato with cheese and chives, house dressin' on the salad."

I guess you do the same thing with it that you do with a hog's bladder or a turkey's or a snake's, if they've got one: you throw it away. Long gone are the days when some great unwritten code required you to keep and put to use every part of a slaughtered animal. As neighbor Bob's neighbor, Mr. Pate, says, "Buzzards got to eat too." What was I going to do, make a water jug out of it the way the Plains Indians did out of buffalo bladders? Not a chance, not when I had a stainless-steel army canteen. And even if I summoned the nerve to tie off the bladder and put my lips to it and blow it full of air, *my* kids sure wouldn't play with it. They'd want something from Walmart.

So I just told him: "Nothing."

"Can I have it?"

It was the same tone of quiet urgency somebody across the table would use asking for the piece of prime steak you've been eating the less savory meat from around, saving it for last—the way some people do. His knife was steady, keen, blood all the way up on the handle, and still pointing at my bladder.

Could he have it? Well, when a fellow asks you whether he can have something you're about to throw away, you just naturally grow cautious, even if he's got a sharp knife six inches from your throat. You don't want to loosen your grip until you know for sure that you're not making a big mistake. It's the same care you have to take at a garage sale. You drag out of the shop or attic something that you are absolutely certain isn't worth the effort it would take to burn or bury, toss it on the bargain table, price it at a dollar, and somebody snatches it up. Then you hear him say to a friend on the way down the drive, "Do you know what this *is?* I seen one for a hundred bucks in a antique store in Houston one time and just about *bought* it. And that damned fool. . . ." The voice trails off—you're too busy scrambling to reassess everything to hear how he concludes.

But back to the bladder. What if Sika urine were now an ingredient in expensive cologne and worth five hundred bucks an ounce at some Paris perfumery, or a South American doctor had discovered that a thimble of it taken daily would shrink hemorrhoids or a swollen prostate, or a sexologist in Europe had developed from it an anti-impotency elixir advertised in *Hustler* and *Penthouse* and *Popular Mechanics?* (And if you think *PM* doesn't run ads on ED, think again. Guys and their tools, you know.) What did this fellow want with that little bag of waters?

So, with the bladder still hanging in the Sika among the other pinks and purples, wiring and plumbing intact, I just up and asked him, "What *for?*"

"Well," he said, his eyes secretive, "what I do is I tie it off and take it to the field with me, and when I establish my blind. . . ." They are so bloody serious about this business, the bowhunters. *Establish* his blind. Like you'd *establish* a new world order or a wartime beachhead or a trust fund for your kids. He'd heard it somewhere. "When I establish my blind, you know, I sprinkle the stuff all around it and on my clothes, dab some on my neck."

"You deliberately put deer piss on yourself?"

"Yeah. You know, it kills the human scent, better'n bakin' soda or oranges or any kind of product that Walmart or Academy sells."

I turned back to my carcass again, thinking *so what if it does?* So you make your blind smell like a Sika buck's *latrine.* What kind of draw is that? Bruce, Bambi's mate or live-in or countergender or whatever you'd call him these days, is bopping along and he smells the stuff and thinks, "Hey, I rekkin I'll go over and check this ol' boy out." Naw. Won't happen. I know all about the territory matter, and maybe deer are different. I tend to shy away from anything that smells like a urinal unless I really need one.

Winter's the mischief in me (and spring, summer, and fall), so I stood back from the Sika and after noting that my right cheek was colder than the left and I was facing south—that meant the wind had to be from the west—I walked a few feet east and relit my cigar, which during the skinning and gutting I'd let go out, and walked back to where he was standing. I don't smoke them often, but gutting any kind of animal liberates smells you far prefer cigar smoke to.

"Look here," I said. "There's an easier way." I blew smoke toward him, and it tumbled back on me.

He just stood there.

"Can you smell my cigar?"

He held his nose in the air, worked it around some. "No."

"No, you cannot," I said. "And if I had slathered on half a cup of cologne—which I would never do because I don't wear the stuff, even to parties—you couldn't smell it. What does that tell you? What fundamental fact of deer hunting are you observing here?"

After a few seconds he said, "I don't know." Then: "I don't smoke cigars. And I sure as hell don't wear cologne when I hunt."

I narrowed my eyes and studied him long and hard, then walked over to my Sika, where I reached in and separated the bladder from the rest of the entrails, cut and tied it off, and handed it to him. "Merry belated Christmas," I said, "enjoy your golden shower."

The Day the Sharpshooter Killed Something He Didn't Intend To

I've been shooting a lot lately, so I have gunpowder on the brain.

While I was painting some shelving boards for the shop the other day, I happened to glance over at an ammunition can full of 30-06 rounds and got to thinking about the time a friend of mine from the army came visiting, and we went out and shot a Springfield '03 I had recently purchased.

This was a long time ago and back in Mississippi, and I was living with my first wife, not that any of this is germane to this piece. It just sets the stage a little.

We loaded up my Rambler station wagon—I *told* you it was a long time ago—and drove down to a place I shot at often, only two or three miles from where I grew up. It was a run-down piece of sorry ground, swampy and snarled with vines and underbrush and lying in the same floodplain my folks' house sat on, so I figured that nobody would mind if I shot there. And I didn't particularly care. Likely as not, any damage I did would be an improvement.

We hiked on back into the woods a little way to a lane I had cleared with an axe: a corridor maybe twelve feet wide and a hundred yards long. The only thing in the background was more woods, so an errant round would be snuffed out fairly quickly. I laid the Springfield down and set up a target, and we sent fifty or sixty rounds downrange before calling it quits.

This is where the story starts.

When we got back to the Rambler, I was sliding the rifle into the back when my friend—let's call him George Stubbs for lack of a better name—looked across and down the road.

"Whose place is that? Looks like something out of *Tobacco Road.*"

And it did. There was a small house, once painted but now a drab gray from the weather, and a run-down barn, junk scattered everywhere. An old black car sat in front of the house, and behind the car a tractor was propped up on concrete blocks.

"At's Hoss Scofield's (name changed) place. Why?"

"Whut kinda car's that anyhow? A Plymouth or something?"

I shrugged. "Or something, I figger."

"Look at that hood ornament. Whut *is* that thang? Big as my fist."

"I'll check it out."

I reached and pulled out my binoculars and studied the car a few seconds. "It's a swan."

I handed the glasses to him, and he confirmed my sighting.

We sat back on the tailgate then and had a beer and started talking about good shooting.

"You know," he said, "my granddaddy was the best shot I ever knew. He was a sniper in WW I and used a rifle kinda like this'n, only it had a weird-shape bolt. Had a scope, too."

"Probably an Enfield," I said. Then: "I wanted to be a sniper, but I just didn't get around to it."

"Whutever it was, he could sure's hell shoot it."

"He ever kill anybody?"

"Nope. Shot the head off a rooster on top of a barn in France—he said they eat good *that* night."

"I don't guess a rooster gets you a Medal of Honor."

George grinned big. "He used to set on his front porch—had a house up near Millport, and it looked down onto Highway 50, which was maybe as far as from here to that guy's house over there. He'd set on his front porch with his that rifle, which somehow he managed to brang back with him from the war took apart in a foot locker, and ever so often he'd take target practice on cars on the highway."

"*What?*"

"Hell, yeah, he'd pick out one with a big ol' hood ornament, like the one over there, and he'd blow it clean off the car. Get hisself a nice lead, with proper elevation for that long range, and shoot that ornament right off the car. He could kill crows *flyin'.*"

"Get back to the ornament story. If that highway was as far from your granddaddy's house as Scofield's place there, you're talking about maybe two hundred yards."

"At least. I mean, you know how distances are to a kid, but it was a long damn way."

"And he'd knock the hood ornaments off cars driving down that highway?"

"He said he missed a couple of times is all, musta busted around thirty or forty."

"What did the people do? I mean, the ones driving the cars that he shot the ornaments off of?"

"They'd stop and get out and study that nekkid hood and shake their heads and wonder, I guess, just whut the hell happened to their swan or goose or elk, or whutever they'd been follerin'. Granddaddy'd scoot back inside after firin' and watch'm from the window. They'd look around and shake their heads some more and then get in and drive off. One time Granddaddy was down at the feed store, and a guy was tellin' about how he was drivin' along out there on the highway and his hood ornament exploded. BAM! Just a puff of silvery dust. Them thangs is made out of pot metal or sumthin, and a bullet just blows'm up like they was glass. Granddaddy slacked off a little after that. Said the heat was on."

"Never got caught?"

"Nope. Never did. Word got out that that particular stretch of highway was hell on ornaments."

George studied the Scofield place a couple of minutes and then said, "I bet I could knock the ornament off that hood over there. A'course, it ain't movin', but. . . ."

"Are you nuts? That's *Hoss Scofield*'s car you're talking about shooting the swan off of."

"So?"

Now, all things considered, Hoss Scofield was not really all that bad. He was known to be a family man in his earlier years, and word is that he tithed sporadically to a little church up near Steens, which he attended on Easter and Christmas. He did not give a full 10 percent of his money to any entity, not even the guvment, which he despised with unrelenting passion, convinced as he was that eventually they would take his guns and vehicles and farm, a euphemism for the squalid, swampy ten-acre place he owned. Nobody could ever reason with him over that issue.

It was rumored that he made "family size" batches of corn likker in a still hidden back in a copse of pines behind his barn, but I never confirmed this. I snooped around all over this property when I was growing up, and I never found a still. I found lots of watermelons though, some of which I claimed, since they didn't have his name on them.

What was not a rumor was that he tolerated no insult to himself or kin or the Confederacy, proudly represented by a rebel flag that hung from a cane pole at the corner of his house, a euphemism for the paintless swayback shack he and his bovine wife lived in. To avoid appearing unkind, one needed a full quiver of euphemisms when describing property belonging to Hoss.

He was known far and wide as someone you did not want to cross under any circumstances and especially when he had been drinking, which was often—or so the rumor went.

I didn't try to keep up with his shenanigans, but he was stuff enough of legend that some stories stuck with me, this one especially, but I'll relate it in more sophisticated fashion than I did to George that day.

Hoss was known to frequent the favors of a waitress at a beer joint a few miles out Highway 50. She did not fall into the category of gorgeous . . . or cute . . . or OK . . . or plain . . . or, well, I think you recognize the direction I'm headed. Succinctly put, her attributes might well have been better registered on a cotton scale than a beauty scale. This is still euphemistic.

It was not that Hoss felt there was much promise in their future, but he was not prepared for the way she chose to dump him: rudely, without ceremony, and without just cause, announcing her intentions before flanking buddies at the bar.

"You and me're finished, you miserable old fart," she had said through the smoky air, adding a puff of her own in his face.

The lights, hanging from the ceiling on slender rods, reeled like constellations in the mirror before him (my description here, since Hoss was probably about as lyrical in thought as he was in speech, right at the level of your average mule) as he stared at her, trying to fix his eyes on her soul, but the windows were not open, so he simply laughed and told his buddies he was leaving. Which he did. Except that he went no farther than the parking lot, where he relieved himself and cursed his fate, and then walked to his truck and removed from the bed a shovel. On entering the bar, he swung wildly until every dangling light was shattered across floor and bar and pool table, leaving a wasteland of glass and plastic shards upon which his heavy boots crunched mightily, and only the garish glow of the neon beer signs lit the way for those who elected to leave. Which was everyone, including the bar owner and her. They slid around the walls and one by one sprang through the door into the night air, staying well out of range of his flailing shovel. Word got out that he was the fastest shovel slinger in the state.

The court was kind. The justice ordered him to pay for the lights and new felt for the pool table, which his shovel had gashed. Apologies all around, and the next Friday night he was at the bar again but without the shovel. She consented to talk quietly with him in his truck about their problem, which he did not even perceive as a problem, namely that he never took her anywhere socially, not even to a Pizza Hut over in Columbus, only to bed, *hers* at that.

"Well, I can't exactly take you to mine, can I?" he asked her. "My wife's usually in it."

This conversation was relayed by the woman to friends, who passed it along to anyone who would listen. The upshot is that they made up that night, but it "take'n for only a week," as Hoss is reported to have said.

(If some of the above sounds a little lyrical, it is perhaps because I described the same scene in a story called "The Pond" [in my second book of short fiction, *Islands, Women, and God*]; indeed the protagonist of that story is based on Hoss, filtered through my memory into fiction. I simply cut the section from the story and pasted it into this piece, with a few minor adjustments here and there. The rest is not from that story.)

The second time they broke up, it was for good. Without leaving him so much as a good-bye note, she hopped a bus and headed west, settling somewhere in Louisiana near her folks.

In his anguish Hoss set fire to the beer joint the night after she left, but after the first whiff of smoke in the bathroom, patrons spewed bottles of beer on the flames until they were snuffed. He was not jailed for the arson, since it was obviously a crime of passion, but he did have to pay for repairs to the bathroom, and he was ordered never to set foot in the joint again.

Over the years Hoss was constantly in trouble with the law: five counts of assault and battery, one count of *theft* of a battery, one count of attempted murder (a shovel blade to the head of a store owner who accused him of stealing a can of Spam), and five charges of DWI (which resulted, finally, in the suspension of his license, of no great consequence to him since he just started driving his tractor [no license required in Mississippi] wherever he needed to go).

"So," I wrapped it up with George, "you are talking about shooting the hood ornament off the car of a man who would as soon kill you as spit downwind. Bad ass of the county."

He listened to all I had to say, then asked, "Rekkin is he there?"

"Truck's gone, so probably not. His wife might be, though. I say we go on home and forget about—"

"Sorry, but I got a point to prove."

Then he reached down and pulled the Springfield out of the car, fished a round out of a box, and loaded the rifle.

"I'm gonna need a rest for this one," he said.

"Hoss catch you, and you'll be resting for eternity."

George walked around to the front of the car and dropped his elbows onto the hood, took his position, adjusted the sight for elevation.

"Yessir, you about to see some chromeyum fly."

"All right, fool, go ahead and take a shot, but you better be ready to haul ass because this Rambler is going to be a mile down the road before the sound of that rifle dies out."

OK, get the picture: George is splayed across the hood of my Rambler, ready to take out a hood ornament. . . .

Three deep breaths. Steady—oh, he was steady.

"Wait a minute."

"Whut?"

"I'm gonna watch this through the glasses."

He relaxed while I fished the binoculars from the car. I took a position right behind him and told him to go ahead and take his shot.

He started the breathing sequence again, and midway through his fourth breath, he fired.

"Ohhhhhh," was all I could manage for a few breaths. "Oh, my God!"

George lifted up and looked at me.

"So I missed the ornament. Big deal. I could barely see it. Ain't no scope on this thang."

"It's not what you *missed.* It's what you *hit.*"

"Gimme them glasses." He snatched the binoculars from me and trained them on the car.

"Whut'd I hit? I don't see nothin'."

"Lift the glasses. Look out beyond the hood of that car about a hundred yards."

"I don't see nothin' but a tracture."

"Precisely. Look at the engine block, about halfway down."

He studied the tractor through the glasses a few seconds.

"It's a big old hole in the side of the block is all I see. Look like it got hit by a bazooka."

"Naw, it got hit by a 30-06 round. That's cast iron, fool, brittle as glass, brittle as the pot metal that hood ornaments are made out of, brittle as peanut, uh, brittle."

"You got any more *brittle as* ideas?"

"They're called *similes.*"

"Yeah, they *would* be, wouldn't they? Ain't whut I'd call'm. Just *goofy* is whut I'd call'm."

"The point is, George, you don't make a neat damn hole in cast iron with a bullet, especially when it's that thin shit in the middle of the block."

"And whut makes you thank I done it?"

"Because I *saw* it, fool. You ran that rear sight up too high, and that bullet smacked into the thin cast iron on that block. You just killed a tractor. He'll have to put a new engine in it."

"I never shot that high, Paul. I—"

"Yes, hell, you did. I saw that plate-size chunk disappear from the engine block when you shot. You missed the ornament by at least two feet. How much do you think a 30-06 drops at three hundred yards? That's not a shotgun slug or a rock. How much did you ramp up that sight?"

"Too much, I rekkin."

"I'll say. Now let's get our recta out of here. I don't think anybody's home, but I don't want to be here when they get back."

"Whut the hell's a rec-tah?"

"It's plural for *rectum,* fool."

He slammed his door and looked back toward Hoss's place. "You ain't gon' never let me forget that you went to college, are you?"

"Nope. Coulda said *ani,* I rekkin, but I don't think that's right. It's been many a year since I took Latin. Let me put it this way, as in Southern Polite. We'd better haul our asses out of here."

"Damn thang is up on blocks anyhow," George mouthed as I drove out the back side of the Sand Road loop.

"Maybe so, but it is *his* tractor on *his* blocks on *his* property. And it's got a washtub-size hole in the engine block."

"Gettin' bigger by the minute, ain't it?"

"All he needed was to put the wheels back on. Now he can put all the wheels on it he wants, and it still ain't going anywhere unless he pushes it or pulls it behind his truck. Gotta buy a whole new engine." I looked over at him. "And, man, is he gon' be bad hacked. He'll put your *ass* up on blocks or blow a hole in it the size of—."

"He'll prolly never even notice it."

"If you had a tractor—even if it was up on cement blocks—wouldn't you notice a hole in the side of your engine block big enough for two possums to nest in?"

"Well, I seen it way back there by the woods, but my sight was on that ornament."

"Yeah, the front sight might have been on it. You probably had that damned elevation set for eight hundred yards."

"I was a sharpshooter in the army, as you well know, so. . . ."

"So was I. But we're not in the army now, and this is not Fort Jackson, South Carolina, and we've both forgot a lot. You're about to know what it was like to be one of those silhouette targets we used to shoot at."

"You really *scarin'* me. . . ." His tone was sarcastic, and he was fake shivering.

"You *better* be scared. You see an old green Dodge pickup cruisin' your neighborhood, you better get outta town. You see so much as the *shadow* of a shovel, and you better duck."

"I ain't scared of no old man with a shovel."

"Famous last words." I looked at him hard. "Did you know that more people have been killed with shovels than have died from cherry bombs exploding in their mouths?" I don't know where that came from, but he didn't say anything in response, so I made *some* kind of point.

I haven't heard from George in years, but I know that even to this day he has nightmares about being hammered to death by a shovel wielded by an old man in overalls yelling over and over, "You kilt my tracture, boy, you kilt my *tracture!*"

Hi-Ho, Hi-Ho, Off to the Gun Show We Go . . .

Billy Wayne Takes in the Gun Show

Lest there be some confusion with the living or the dead, I have changed the names of the people in this piece—instead of using Willard, the actual name on the fellow's coveralls and tattoo, I have used Billy Wayne, and the girl's name on the tattoo has been changed from Tammy to Lynelle; to be extra safe, I have changed the flower color on the tattoo from violet to orange. Publishers are very sensitive about the use of actual names and descriptions in pieces.

Billy Wayne knows only that what he's holding in his hand is a gun that was probably made long before he was born and is likely to rust away to nothing before he ever reads a book. He is in fact holding an Enfield Martini, made famous by British troops during the Anglo-Zulu War of the late nineteenth century, but it is not a fact that concerns him—he is disturbed that the chamber is too large for a .410 and too small for a twenty gauge, and every military cartridge he knows anything about slides way down into the bore. In short Billy Wayne cannot shoot his gun, and this troubles him no end. What if terrorists attacked his trailer?

His name is sewn in white on a dark-blue oval patch on the back of his coveralls, which are a dark-striped lighter blue with old and new grease smudges on them, which means, I 'spect, that he does not work in upper management. I will assume that his name is on his back so that others will know what to call him, or so that he can tell his coveralls from someone else's, should he for some reason leave them hanging somewhere. For self-identification he needs merely to glance at the tattoo on his wrist, where his name is emblazoned on a blue ribbon that threads through the fangs of a large-mouth snake wreathed in vines with orange flowers dotting them. A smaller ribbon, pink, with *Lynelle* on it, dangles from the snake's lower jaw.

I have spent enough time in the halls of academe that I should be able to decipher the symbolism, but Billy Wayne would have to be still awhile for me to do it, and it takes a special need to ask someone with a gun—especially someone who looks like him—to hold still while you study his arm.

I want to tell him about the rifle, but the tall man dressed in khaki he's talking to, before whom a table ripples with lever-action Winchesters on blue velvet, is doing it for me, patiently explaining that the Martini will not accommodate any cartridge that Billy Wayne has ever seen and that if by chance one did lodge in the chamber within striking distance of the firing pin, to pull the trigger on it would probably be supreme folly. Understanding man that he is, he does not phrase it this way to Billy Wayne. He puffs up his cheeks, holds his hands to them, then expels the air with an explosive sound, carrying his hands out as wide as he can fling them, suggesting that his fingers might be disconnected pieces of Billy Wayne's face—nose, ears, eyes, lips, etc. Billy Wayne nods *unh-hunh* and moves on down the line, where eventually I lose sight of him. If the Martini did not look like it had been used to drive steel fence posts in bad weather, he might well sell it.

My bet is that Billy Wayne will end up trading his tortured Martini and a hundred dollars for another exotic, say a Russian Nagant revolver with machining so crude you can sharpen an axe or saw through jail bars with the barrel and currently selling for sixty-five dollars through *Gunlist* and *Shotgun News.* He will take it home and try to fit .38 Specials into it, and if that won't work—and it won't, not by a long shot—he'll hang it on a wall for show or use it to weight a trotline, which is what he should have done with the Martini. But that's Billy Wayne's problem, not mine. Then too, I could be wrong about the outcome. Anything can happen here.

Billy Wayne, along with a few thousand other souls, is at the gun show in the Astrohall, where several times a year the Houston Antique Gun Dealers Association holds its big fling, one of the largest in the country. These dealers are not out to skin anybody, but neither will they turn down a hide if it's salted and dried and folded and handed to them. They are only human, no matter how the media and gun-control people might argue otherwise.

I have pounded the concrete aisles for four hours, enough time to examine only a third or so of the more than two thousand tables—laden with guns, clips (magazines, if you prefer), reloading tools and components, knives, and books—and exhibits spread out in rows across the hall. It is a two-day job if done properly.

At the moment I am sitting high in a plush chair (as plush as they get here—all the others are folding metal) scribbling notes while my shoes are being shined. They are work shoes, I have told the shineman, but he says that he will put a high gloss on them, no matter what. They will look like polished *work* shoes, I tell him, but he smiles and whirls his brush and rag. With unforked tongue I can say that I do not care what they look like when he's through, anymore than I cared what they looked like when I came in. I am in his chair and paying five dollars for a shine so that I may rest the feet inside those shoes. I've already timed him, and it takes twelve to fifteen minutes for him to get the shine he wants. With these shoes, maybe twenty. Whatever, it's worth the five dollars. I have advised him that I will give him another five for a martini, one with an olive in it.

"Not at the gun show," he says, smiling. "Unless you want to go with me out to the truck, where I gots some shonuff white lightnin'."

I decline.

When I'm through here and the shineman asks me to make room for the next customer, I'm going over into the antiques section of the hall to browse—that's where the women hang out while the men prowl the gun-show aisles—and maybe find something interesting. (I am eclectic in taste.) Who knows, Lynelle might be over there, not that I would know her from any other woman, unless she's got a tattoo that says *Billy Wayne* on it. I could always yell out "Lynelle" and duck, see who turns. But such nonsense is chancy at a place like this, with ol' Billy Wayne walking around shouldering a Martini club. Besides, Lynelle is probably two thousand miles away from here, married to an upper manager, and has forgotten all about the fool that put her name on a tattoo, if she ever knew him.

Boram

I decided that the name Rambo for our macho man might be a little hackneyed, so I changed it to Boram, pronounced Bow-Ram. *It does sound supercharged with testosterone, doesn't it, the bow and ram being ancient instruments of war? Further, it sounds biblical, even apocalyptic. (No confusion with bowhunters is intended.)*

Another time and place, armed as he is with a brace of pistols and something that looks like an Uzi dangling from a sling, folks would dive for the nearest cover to hide until Boram shambled away to another county. For this is, as they say in the movies, *one bad dude,* not a man to mess with. He looks like an Anglicized, modernized Pancho Villa: broad and ponderous of stature, eyes cold gray balls of steel swinging back and forth in their slits, blond mustache constantly atwitch like some animal testing the wind. His hair has been shorn to short stubble, and the back of his head has a broad-lipped meaty smile between the crown and shoulders, perhaps somewhere on the neck; I cannot be certain where his neck begins and ends, but I can tell you its color: deep red. The back of his head smiles more than the front. I am reminded of the back of the head of a football coach I hated in high school—one night at the fair I flung half a candied apple right toward the middle of his tailgate smile. (It is better not to name him, since he might still be dangerous.) I pretended it was a grenade but did not wait around to hear it explode.

Boram wears camelflogged—I really do know the proper spelling, but a student of mine spelled it this way once, and I kinda liked it—pants, bloused above scarred black combat boots, and an olive T-shirt that has printed on the front his solution for the world's undesirables: "Kill 'em all and let God sort 'em out." He is not thinking about fire ants and mosquitoes. On the back he has worried out in black Magic Marker the words *White Power* and beneath that the letters *AB,* which could stand for *Aryan Brotherhood* or merely serve as evidence that he has made some initial progress in his attempt to learn the alphabet.

The pistols—which look like a Colt 1911 and Beretta, though, like cars these days, it's hard to tell at a distance—are held in place by the same belt that keeps the upper part of his belly from avalanching and compounding his more than ample middle. The little submachine gun, I'd hope semiautomatic, just looks *mean.* He carries a nylon bag on the opposite side from the sub; I doubt that it bulges with Bibles or knitting.

He may be selling, he may have just bought, or he may simply be on parade, dressed bad, dressed to kill, to have his day, the only place he can do it without someone calling the police. The men in blue at the door are supposed to have determined that he has no ammunition on board, and they have run little plastic ties between the frame and hammer of the pistols and through the receiver on the sub; so, if you like, you may make an obscene gesture at him and not fear a riddling from his heavy metal. But there is the question of what's in his bag (undeactivated grenades? a clutch of charged magazines?) and always the wide parking lot to cross afterwards, so I keep my tongue in my cheek and my finger where it belongs. Sticking out your tongue or flinging him a finger could be an easy suicide, as certain a way as any, perhaps swifter and more resolute than to unfurl a finger in Houston traffic.

This is a man who longs for Armageddon, who has plotted many times over the scenarios he will follow when, as the poet Yeats put it, the center cannot hold and "anarchy is loosed upon the world, / The blood-dimmed tide is loosed. . . ." It is coming, the blood-dimmed tide, he has told himself, and he will make it through, he will *survive.* He hopes only that when things give way, he will be at his trailer home, mobile and ready to haul it to the mountains. I am only guessing here, but I can imagine it bristling with guns of every sort, so that should the enemy be a cool, distant speck on the landscape or a hot savage breath upon him, he will have the proper weapon. I can even fancy a rotating turret on the roof, a fifty-caliber barrel protruding from it, trained on the horizon.

As he shuffles down the aisles glancing right and left, the stream of people parts for him, flows to either side, joins again behind, some looking back and grinning and rolling their eyes, others intent on their business. Boram makes the corner to stalk another aisle, and I lose sight of him in the crowd.

Perhaps I have been unkind to this fellow, for some mother brought him into this world and still loves her big boy, pinches his cheeks, coos over him as she serves his favorite dessert. He is yet the apple of her eye. It may be that he is as gentle to the core as the pudge he was at three, jostling on his father's knee and drooling. In a burst of Christian charity let us believe this of him in closing: that he is a Jesuit in training, a gentle peacemaker playing a role to help him better understand the people he may someday be called on to minister to, assuaging their fears, soothing their savage spirit.

The Women of the Gun Show

Most of the people at the gun show are ordinary *men,* sensible and sane and conservative to moderate in their political leanings. Some hunt, some collect, some target shoot, some reload, some do all of these; but like gun-control advocates, they would keep guns out of the hands of those who would misuse them and insist on severe punishment for those who commit a crime with a firearm. And they cringe at the prospects of a world roamed by Borams, whom they would have caged and fed daily a ration of carrots and Prozac. Businessmen, professors, carpenters, doctors, lawyers, butchers, bakers, candlestick makers (fairly rare these days)—they are all there, looking and touching and buying often enough that the dealers keep coming back. I go because I like to look at the guns and study the people. On a per-hour cost basis, it's the cheapest good entertainment I can think of.

Man's world though the gun show may be, a few women roam the aisles, almost always with their boyfriends or husbands, sometimes pushing babies in buggies, and women women tables. (I must assume that if a man mans a table, a woman *womans* it.) Even behind the table, though, the woman is usually with her husband or live-in, her countergender (pun intended).

Viewed by ravening feminists, the women of the gun show compliantly follow in the wake of their men like hollow shells adrift in their wake. "It is in their blood and tiny brains to do it, these weaker ones," they would say with contempt. "They do not have the backbone to resist. They would follow their men into hell."

And a gun-show woman would answer, "It's none of your business, but sometimes we *do* follow them into hell. Or halfway there. And we will again and again. It makes the going easier for them, and more often than not we can drag them back. Those who came before us, generations ago, followed them across the great water and over mountains and through swamps and rivers, fire and flood, wherever they wanted to go. We follow them, as we always will, no matter their purpose or passion, for we know that without us the world would plunge into chaos and end by morning. And let me add this, you constipated bitches: at least I have my man."

No man has made them come here. No arm has been twisted. They come by choice. And this choice is dictated by common sense. They are, in fact, guardians of the financial realm, moderators of male passion for guns and knives and swords. They temper the appetite for ordnance (*ordnanism,* if you will). Without these calm heads along, the men would walk out with truckloads of guns, taking out second and third mortgages, signing promissory notes running well into the next decade, and putting up the titles to their trucks and boats and cars.

Hefting this nice Winchester '73, holding it out at arms' length, our typical husband says, "Lord, just look at it, Honey. Can't you just see that hanging on the wall above the mantle?"

"No, I cannot, Jack," the wife answers. "What I can see is twelve hundred dollars worth of furniture for the den that mantle is in. Gallery's running a sale on oak."

"I've always wanted one of these. It's in NRA excellent condition, bore's almost mint. Just look down that barrel." He has dropped the lever and inserted a bore light.

"No woman wants to look down the barrel of a gun, Jack. Talking *about* a bore. You look down that bore if you want to, then put the rifle back." She may even be secretly surprised at the rhyme.

"But the price is right, Sweetheart. Look at the *lines.*"

"Think *bottom* line, Jack. Look at the *line* of Gertrude's teeth when we get home. They're like two benches full of strangers in her mouth—half her upper teeth have never met them on the bottom. You and me never got braces, but *she's* going to have them."

"I got a little bit of extry money coming in from that valve job down in Bay City—"

"Little bit is right. Where's the other half coming from? The den furniture or the down payment on Gertrude's teeth is where. Just look at the gun, Jack, *feel* of it. Then put it back down on the green velvet, where it really looks nice. You don't want to leave a gap on the man's table."

"Ma'am," the dealer says, springing to his feet, "I got three more—"

The look she gives him would freeze dry dirt. He shrugs and sits back down, stares at his hands.

"Hold it, Jack. Feel it and look at the pretty gun. Then put it back on the table. We don't *need* that thing."

He lifts and aims the rifle, works the lever, admires once again the fine craftsmanship that went into the walnut and steel, then lays it on the table and turns away, eyes wistful. She squeezes his arm, tiptoes, kisses him on the cheek. She has led him once again out of temptation.

Without his woman along, Jack would have bought the Winchester, the hell with den furniture and Gertrude's crooked teeth. And he would have faced unholy hell when he got home with it. There would have been an appalling fight with his mate that might or might not have known any reasonable bounds—he could have found himself later that night with a wad of blankets in the back of his pickup and that cold darling, Winnie Chester, to sleep with.

The women of the gun show fascinate me. I watch them sometimes, the pretty and the plain, and wonder what goes through their heads as they slowly walk the aisles beside their men, what they are dreaming of, what lines they are rehearsing to head off the next attempt to buy. This is not their tea—bag, cup, or crock. Their eyes declare the same dreadful boredom I used to feel in Foley's or Dillard's when I tagged along beside my wife shopping for women's clothes. Though tedium settles over their faces like dust by midafternoon, in their eyes I see a scintilla of hope, like sunlight behind heavy clouds. They know that no vigil is eternal, no pain goes on forever.

From "Growing Up in Mississippi Poor and White but Not Quite Trash"

(An As-Yet-Unpublished Memoir)

Trains

The Beginning of a Lifelong Quest for Understanding

All through my first years of memory in the little hamlet of Millport, Alabama, where I was born, there were trains. Chuffing, blaring, clacking trains. Great black trains with billowing smoke and noise to wake the dead. Days and nights they ran through my head as I waited for them, timing by the sun if I timed at all—I *knew* when they were coming. I felt them before I heard, felt the earth tremble or the house, the faint shimmer of windows that nobody else seemed to notice, felt something as real as the drumming of my blood begin and swell, and then I could see the column of gray-black smoke by day, sometimes laid almost flat by speed and the wind, or from my bed see the slash of the headlight split the dark. And then the noise, the wonderful noise of that massive engine and its string of colorful cars.

I knew when it was going to stop in Millport and when it was blasting on through. I knew from the urgency of the tremor, from the sound of the engine as it drew closer to town, from the way the engineer blew his horn. Nights I didn't care whether it stopped or not, because once I was in bed there was no leaving the house, but days I tore toward the tracks the instant I knew it was coming.

My grandparents' house was two blocks south of the tracks, on the proper side—there was a planing mill on the other side—and three blocks west, along the street that ran parallel to the railroad, was the Cities Service station that my grandfather operated: a white building with green trim, two gas pumps, a grease ramp, and a rack of tires. My earliest recollections of Millport come from the service station: the smell of old tires and gasoline and oil, the clanging of tools, and the incredible food my grandfather cooked there. For years they lived in that building before the moved into the house.

But no matter what was happening at the station, when the train was due to arrive, night or day, my grandfather would roll away the tire he was working on or lay down his wrench, leave a car's sump half filled with oil, and turn off the stove. The train was more important.

Across the street from the service station was the depot, the only name I ever knew it by, where passengers loaded and disembarked and cargo and mail were exchanged. My grandfather delivered the mail from the depot to the post office, a couple of blocks away. He knew by heart the schedules, and rain or shine he was there with his two-wheeled wooden cart waiting when the locomotive panted up and the brakes squealed it to a stop in a cloud of steam, the cars gently bumping each other in a little game of tag all the way back to the red caboose, tiny in the distance. A man in a dark uniform tossed the gray canvas bags down to Mr. Shade, as my grandfather was called, and he stashed them in his cart and trotted out of sight.

The trains then were fired with coal, not much of an evolution from the horridly noisy, nasty woodburning engines of a decade or so before, perhaps not as clunky looking, but just as sooty, a universe removed from the sleek, bright diesels that came a few years later. The engine was enormous, built for power, black and practical, with nothing adorning it except for the bell, usually made of brass, and a copper whistle, always polished. Its components seemed to me to be the fashionings of giants. Surely mortal men could never manage such enormous riveted plates, ponderous rails, and bars and piping, vast steel wheels tall as the boy who studied them. Even sitting still the engine throbbed with energy, straining to be on the way again, like some great black beast happy with its lot, glad to pull for the men who fed it. Once I sat in an engine that had been sidetracked for minor repairs, and a great sadness came over me in that cold cab with its monstrous levers and gauges, the door of hell itself cool to the touch. A light wind blew through and moaned around the window openings. A bird sailed in and fluttered as if to land, then left through the opening on the other side. It was just not right. The bird knew and I knew. It was the sadness I felt in my grandmother's kitchen when everyone had left it for the day—a place without purpose, its energy gone.

Immediately behind the engine came the humpback coal car mounded with lumps of black fire to keep the boilers going. The fireman who worked in it, who shoveled and shuttled coal from car to fiery furnace, was forever sooty, a smudged Vulcan caught between the outer world of fresh air and blue sky and the yawning door of hell beneath the boiler. Summer or winter, this man never smiled. Never in my whole memory does a smiling coal man come into focus. When I see his teeth, I see them through a snarl. His was not, I think, a happy job. My grandfather warned me away from the coal car because of the gritty coal dust that clung to anything that came near it—he did not wish a scolding from my mother for soiled clothes—and because of the surly coal man.

After the coal car was the mail car, a mysterious enclosed boxcar whose forward end was coated with heavy black as if it had nosed through pitch. It was plated with steel and had heavy riveted doors and a small sliding window through whose barred opening someone inside could see out but no one outside could see in or enter. I once watched a mirror, delicate-handled and silver and ornate like a lady's, creep out through the bars and pivot this way and that to make certain, I suppose, that no robbers were about. Then the big door slid open, only slightly, and a pale man dressed in dark blue squeezed through and descended, his eyes working beneath the bill of his cap the way the mirror had done—up and down, around. Satisfied there was no threat at hand, he turned and closed and padlocked the door and disappeared into the depot, returning a couple of minutes later with a Coca-Cola in one hand and something in a small brown paper sack in the other. His eyes were still darting about. He clamped the bag under one arm, expertly unlocked and removed the padlock with his free hand, slid the door open just enough, and swung back up into his refuge. The door closed and I heard a bolt slide home.

The passenger cars came next, long and many windowed, then boxcars of yellow or green or red with names and logos of the companies that owned them, then flatcars mounded with coal or grain or timbers, occasionally olive-drab jeeps and trucks. At the rear followed the caboose, second only to the engine in its fascination. Here there were bunks for the crew, a pot-bellied stove whose pipe rose straight up through the roof, and a small table with bench seats where they sometimes took their meals. There were magazines and newspapers stashed everywhere, and the place smelled of cigars and pipes and burning coal.

Once, while playing in the caboose during a train's extended stopover, I discovered beneath a pillow a magazine printed in a foreign language, on the cover an alluring woman whose eyes said *Look inside, little boy, and see something you have never seen before.* The magazine fell open to a page where I saw my first naked woman. For as long as I dared I gazed, awestruck, unbelieving, my brief experience with the mysterious bodies of women limited to what I had seen in the lingerie section of the Sears catalog. But for the fear of a mericiless hell, whose fires my Victorian mother had graphically described to me, I would have stolen that magazine. My head reeling, I shoved it back under the pillow, but in the weeks that followed, the more I thought about it, the more I knew that if I ever had the chance again I would take that magazine, would risk the fiery furnace, though it be hot as the flames beneath the engine boiler, for another glimpse of that woman's secret places.

I knew nothing of airplanes, though I saw and heard a few pass over from time to time, so the trains were my reminder that another world lay out there, from which the tracks came and to which they went at the other end: vast cities of towering buildings that for years I would only read and hear about and see in jittery movies, cities of bumper-to-bumper cars, beautiful women and powerful men, and a lurid life of the flesh, dens of iniquity, as my mother put it. When I saw the smoke approach from the east, looking for all the world as if it were trailing the fury of hell itself, I knew the train was coming from Tuscaloosa and Birmingham, maybe even that magic city Atlanta; when it came from the west, all I could think about was Texas.

In those days a train engineer had the same social status as an airline pilot of today, a hero to every small boy whose heart leapt to see a hand rise from the throttle and wave as the train roared by. He carried himself with full knowledge of his status, did the engineer, and when he condescended to step down from his engine onto the platform, people watched and listened. For he had been places they had never been and might never see, and in his strong hands he held the fate of passengers and freight and mail. He moved silently, his eyes fixed straight ahead, nodding briefly to the ladies and gentlemen, ignoring the children, a man of gravity and dignity whose presence radiated and rippled among us as if from that great rumbling chariot a god had descended. I knew only two engineers during my years there, one aloof and wordless, the other as friendly as an uncle. He was the one who let me sit at the controls and brought me candy. (Those were the days before such kindnesses would be considered suspicious.)

On the passenger trains there was always at least one conductor, who moved from car to car punching tickets and seeing that the customers' needs were met. They wore dark uniforms like the man in the mail car, but theirs had more trim, red or gold, and their black caps were stiff and formal, with shiny black leather bills and bands, unlike those of the coalmen and oilers and engineers, whose soiled and crumpled caps were made of what looked like the cloth mattresses were made of. The conductors must have polished their buttons daily, for they shone like gold, and they were forever brushing their coats and trousers of whatever real or imagined specks had landed there.

One conductor especially intrigued me. A tall, muscular black man, he had a forehead high and stern and would, I thought, have looked down his nose at God. His was a different language from the local blacks, curt and crisp, his teeth flashing boldly when he spoke, though he never smiled. I kept well clear of him, never allowing his red-tinged eyes to meet mine if I could avoid it. Even the engineer and coal man seemed afraid of him. When he said so, the train moved. It stayed stock-still until he did. I wondered often whether my father would have had the nerve to order him to go around to the back door or what my grandfather would have said to him if he drank from the whites' only water fountain at the service station.

As the train sat there in a leisurely pant, the station was a flurry of activity, the most excitement these small towns could have except when the fair was there in September. Passengers scrambled aboard under the cool eye of the conductor while the coal man shoveled and sweated, the engineer checked his gauges, and the oilman moved from bar to rod to wheel, topping the bearing boxes. My grandfather exchanged bags with the man in the mail car, whose pale thin arm always seemed about to break as he hoisted up the outgoing and dropped the incoming.

A few times that one engineer allowed me to sit at the controls of the idling engine, knowing that my small hands could never tug anything into or out of gear. Once he held me up and let me blow the whistle, jolting bolt upright two old men who perpetually occupied a bench outside the station doors. I was more impressed with those few round white-faced gauges of that engine and its five or six simple levers than I would be decades later when I sat in the cockpit of a 747.

I rode on a train only once, the last year of the war, while my father was at Fort McClellan in Anniston, 150 miles away, almost due east. I cannot recall how long the trip took—I was only four—but much as I loved watching the green countryside slide past us as we lurched and shunted throughout a whole day, the sun sliding around in the sky as the track veered to fit the terrain, it was a very long time. Nothing to that point in my life was as opulent as those leather seats trimmed in green, the rich red aisle runner, and sandwiches and sweating mugs of milk served off shiny trays. If the ride had been a week over to Anniston, I could not have slept. I kept wanting to get out of my seat and look at the magazines, just in case . . . but Mother kept me close.

I remember nothing of the stay overnight at Fort McClellan and very little of the trip back. The novelty of the trip having given way to little-boy weariness, I slept most of the way, clutching in my arms a small glass engine that my father had given me, shaped like the one that was pulling us and filled with small hard candies, reds and greens and yellows. For weeks afterwards I shook from its crystal smokestack daily one bright pellet, whose taste reminded me of trains and the worlds they came from and went to. As I sucked them to a lingering sweetness in the back of my throat, I pretended they were dreams.

Learning about Sex

If I had to choose the one subject that occupied my mind more than any other after the age of ten or so, it would have to be sex. Never under this sun was there a child more ignorant of the act, the organs involved, or its marvelous potential for pleasure and fulfillment. And never was there a child who tried harder to understand.

Not having a sister, and living in the country with few close neighbors, I seldom found myself around girls, except for those at school and church. Every boy I knew well had a sister, so they did not have to suffer the torment I did. What was so unfair was that they didn't want to talk about their sisters' private places to me. I mean, they had seen the light, and there I was crawling along in the dark looking for some glimmer.

My mother was so modest about her body that, with the exception of the time I saw her naked in bed with Daddy, with nothing showing in the way of truly female equipment, I never saw anything of it beyond her face and appendages after I was old enough for my mind to record such things. She kept well-covered, indoors and out, so she could have been completely without the usual female equipment, and I would not have been the wiser. (I never saw my father's genitals until one day in the hospital while he was dying—in some sort of delirium he yanked the sheet aside and I saw his penis flopped over like a little dead mouse.)

My parents were, as I described them in the first novel I attempted, as sexless as stumps, and that is not an exaggerated simile. They never mentioned sex at all except for a blanket condemnation of any touching *down there.*

"It's *nasty,*" Mother would say. "That's a *nasty* place. You ain't sposed t'touch yourself there or touch anybody else there or let anybody else touch *you* there. It's *nasty.*" (*Nasty* was the vilest word they seemed to be able to conjure to describe something bad. The way she said the word, I always got visions of sweat and "potato rows" and pus and scabs.)

Once I challenged that admonition by asking her what about taking it out to pee, but she just said, "You know what I mean," even when I really didn't, because I had not made the connection yet, had not launched that rocketship to the stars.

Of course I wondered just exactly what God's punishment would be for touching yourself down there except when you unfurled it to pee. I concluded that the preacher's warning about hell being hotter than your mother's stove and burning you all over and forever applied in this instance too, and I winced thinking about what would get the focus of all that heat. It didn't stop me from fooling with it, but when I was little I always felt guilty and scared when that delicious throbbing went away.

I found then and still find today utterly incredible the notion of my parents making love. Yeah, I know everybody says that, but they don't deep-down mean it—they can see it if they try hard enough and not be repulsed. I can hold my mouth every way I know and twist my mind in all directions, and drunk or stoned or dead sober I cannot fancy those two people coupled in bed or in the backseat of a car or in a hayloft or anywhere else where things like that might happen. When I walked in on them one Sunday afternoon when I was supposed to be off at the river and saw my naked mother lying on top of my naked father in their bed, there was neither sound nor motion. In fact I think that they were asleep. But something had definitely been going on. That image troubled me a long time, though they were sandwiched so tightly that I could see nothing of their private parts.

Now in spite of all her silence and negativity about sex, that grand taboo, my mother did one of the strangest things I've ever known a woman to do: she kept all her used Kotexes in one of those mesh sacks that oranges or grapefruit come in. It hung from a nail on one of the exposed rafters of the pump house, square in the middle of the little building. This one was yellow, so I guess it was a grapefruit bag. She would go out two or three times a day while she was on her period and put the pads in that bag and continue until it filled up; then mysteriously it would disappear, only to reappear with a Kotex or two in it a few weeks later. And she didn't wrap them up in toilet paper the way most women do—she just folded them over like half a tomato sandwich and dropped them in. They would usually spring at least halfway open. The older they were, the darker the patch of blood.

I remember thinking one day that they looked like Lilliputian mattresses on which some small creature had bled. I had read a bit in Swift.

I mean right in the middle of the pump house, where my friends not only could see it but had to dodge to get by it, like a damned punching bag. I had to duck around it every time I went in to take a shower under the barrel mounted on top of the pump house and filled each day for the sun to warm the water, and it loomed there like a sack of horrors anytime I went into the shop, which occupied the front half of the pump house.

What did it mean? I have no idea. I never asked her. Didn't dare. I'm not sure she knew, and I'm relatively certain my father didn't. He never said anything. He just dodged it too. Maybe she was making a statement, demonstrating her suffering perhaps, like Christ on the cross with his open wounds.

I never knew what she did with them when she emptied the bag, whether she took them out and buried them somewhere in the garden or out in the field behind the house or burned them in the rusty trash barrel. All I know is that on a day I would walk into the pump house, and the bag would be hanging up there empty again or with one or two Kotexes in it. I mean, this was before recycling kicked in, and so far as I know, that particular product hasn't made the list yet. Besides, the way my parents felt about the government, if Washington had sent down a decree to recycle air, my parents would have set their minds to figuring out how not to.

It may be that this is something that went on all across the South in those days. I just know that I've never heard anybody else talk about it, and I have not been able to discover on the Internet so much as a whisper of Mother's tradition.

The first glimpse I recall of a girl's most private part was actually among the very first memories lodged deep in the dark of my mind. We were living in a house in Millport, Alabama, on what is now called Columbus Street (and might have been then, for all I know), and this girl named Barbara Ann—yeah, I remember her last name, but I ain't a'tellin'—and I sat beneath a tree and showed each other our "things," but I swear I saw nothing down there on her that registered. Her legs came together and her torso began, and there was a little puffy cleft, like her armpit, but that was all. I was not at all impressed, but I certainly noticed a difference between us.

But for one swift and blinding view of a naked woman in that foreign magazine I found in the caboose of that train, for a long time what I knew of the shape of women I derived principally from one source—the lingerie section of the Sears catalog—which in those days no household would have been without, even if they had indoor plumbing, which we did not for a long time. Oh, the pleasure of studying those pages and pages of women wearing nothing but panties and bras and corsets. So lovely and so vulnerable, they were mine anytime I wanted. Slide the big thick book out, let it fall naturally open to that section, spine sprung as it was within two weeks of its arrival, and they were mine.

Now these women, mind you, wore not the flimsy sorts of undergarments you see in Victoria's Secret. The kind Sears sold were formidable devices, almost medieval in design, and their purpose was to contain and conceal and restrain and reshape, not to lure men, perhaps to physically *repel* them. A study of my mother's underwear revealed much wire and heavy cloth and elastic strong enough to harness a mule or make a slingshot powerful enough to shoot a rock through a concrete block.

But in my mind's eye the garments in the catalog grew gossamer and ethereal and fell away readily from those lovely women of Sears to reveal, to reveal . . . hell, I didn't know, couldn't imagine. I knew more about the economics of Portugal. What I saw in the magazine in Millport that day was unsteady in my mind: I was so awestruck that not much of it lingered in my ready memory. It was like looking at the sun. When you try to recall what it looks like, you can't, even when the image is still dancing deep in your head. It is simply too much light.

The big catalog came twice a year, with a summer supplement, if I remember correctly, courtesy of the U.S. Postal Service, and I never got my hands on it until Mother had thumbed through it, dreaming about all the stuff that she could order, if only she had the money, and sometimes Daddy would have his go at it to look at tools and guns. In those days you could buy surplus firearms for ten bucks or so and new rifles and shotguns for way less than they cost uptown. Finally though, my time came, and I would take the catalog off somewhere private and find the women.

The spring/summer editions had them in bathing suits as well, and sometimes the same model would show up wearing panties and bra in one section and a bathing suit in another. There was one brunette I fell particularly hard for. Flawless of face and limb, she had long hair, straight and very dark, and her eyes seemed to bore right into mine, as if we really knew each other. I would spend hours staring at her, wondering what she was like, what it would be like to touch her, what she looked like with nothing on. I have written a story in which a retired university professor goes off on a quest to find one of these ladies who so brightened his formative years. . . .

Once a catalog was replaced by a new one, the old one migrated to the outhouse, where sheets were randomly torn from it. The first thing I did was tear out the lingerie section, layer the pages in wax paper, and hide them in my grandfather's barn next door, deep in bales of hay, which I formed tunnels in to my own secret places. Along the back wall I always left an opening that I could squirrel through to the light, so that I could study the women of Sears.

Some kid taught me a trick at school. You could take a pencil eraser and delicately remove the ink from a picture in a newspaper, comic book, or catalog and completely take the clothes off Blondie or Veronica or a Sears model, but you had to be really careful not to tear or wrinkle the paper. So it was that I would erase the panties and bra from my brunette (who appeared several years in a row) and try to draw in what I imagined was there. But it was futile. I couldn't imagine something I'd never seen. You have to have frames of reference, you know. So I just guessed. I drew a little slit and shaded in some hair with the side of my lead. (The breasts I never did get even remotely right to suit me, so I usually just left the bra or bathing suit top on.) They might not have been da Vinci–league renderings, in either technique or anatomical correctness, but they served. That is what counts: they *served.*

In time I would replace my frayed pages with newer ones and bury the old ones in the woods—I buried hundreds of women along the river. When I got saved at church, as I did quite frequently, I would always have to dig my women out of the hay and burn them and my comic books in the trash barrel, which seemed to be a fitting way to dispose of sin, but as soon as the salvation wore off, usually within two days unless it *really* took and hung in for a week or more, I would be clawing through the ashes in the barrel to see what I could salvage.

Sometimes there was a long wait for Mother and Daddy to get through with the catalog, so I would slip into my grandmother's house and steal hers. I can still recall hearing the fits she pitched when her catalogs disappeared. It was a terrible loss for any country woman to suffer, and she would tear the house up trying to find it and yell at my grandfather, blame him for doing something with it. The worst part was that once I took one and tore out the lingerie section, I would have to throw the rest of the catalog in the river. I couldn't, after all, return it to her house with those particular pages missing. Somebody would have been in trouble, and you can imagine how long that blame would circle before it landed right square on *my* head.

Until I was almost thirteen, then, I didn't know for real what a girl or woman looked like down there. (Late in my early life, a cousin introduced me to *it.* This was an experience well worth recalling and writing about, but I suspect I'd be better off keeping it to myself.) I might just as well have been guessing the features of the face of God. I had pretty well figured out the general shape of breasts from the caboose magazine and from furtive studies of my teachers and women at church and my Sears ladies, but the magic place was beyond my ken.

The boy who lived next door, Billy Ponds, had a sister, a pretty, magical thing whom I occasionally saw, but, five years or so older than we were, she kept well away from us filthy boys. I tried a few times to glimpse her unclothed through a cracked curtain, but I always chickened out before I got close enough to see anything.

One morning while I was over at Billy's waiting to catch the school bus, I opened the door to one of the back rooms in their small house—this was before they built the larger brick house nearer the street—and walked in on Sarah just as she was pulling on a pair of panties. She was facing the door, absolutely naked, but it was almost as if I had been struck blind again by too much light. She shrieked and spun away from me, and I saw nothing but a dazzle of female limbs and torso, nothing distinct, no more than I could have seen details on the surface of the sun. She was at least fifteen, so her breasts had to have been there, a thatch of hair, but none of it registered. I had seen truth itself and been struck blind again.

This was a problem that needed solving, so I turned to the only source of esoteric knowledge that I thought I could rely on: a particular boy at school who knew about such things. I'll lie and call him Willie, since he still lives over there and might not want his name involved in an unsavory context like this.

Willie lived way out in the country, and he knew just about everything there was to know about things our parents tried their damnedest to keep from us. One day at recess during the fourth grade we were huddled around him at the edge of the playground. He had found a condom dangling on the bike rack that morning and snatched it off and stashed it in his lunch bag. He opened the little brown-paper sack and pulled the condom out the way a magician removes something from his hat, secretively and with style.

"What you reckon that fuckin' rubber was doing on the bike rack, Willie?" someone in the circle asked. For some reason, in those days we always called them "fuckin' rubbers," as if they might have had other purposes, like carrying survival water in, the excuse a friend of mine gave when his wife caught him with a packet while she was pregnant.

"I guess they thought it was a fuckin' rubber rack," Willie said and laughed. We all laughed. He shook it out and examined it in the sun.

"It ain't been used," he said.

"How can you tell?" I asked.

"I can tell," he said. He slid it over a finger and held it up. "Still got the powder on it. Ain't been fired." He laughed again and pitched the rubber onto another kid's arm, where it landed like a snakeskin. The kid squealed and flung it back to Willie. Willie put it in his pocket, said he'd find a use for it later.

"Hey, Willie." I touched him on the arm. "Tell me what a woman looks like down there."

He studied my face a few seconds and squinted as if someone had blown smoke into his face.

"It ain't no way I can just tell you something like that in words. It's a hole with hair around it, but it ain't that simple. More like a slit with hair above and trailing down either side of it, until they spread their legs, and then it gapes open if they are hot and ready."

He looked around our rapt little group, which I figure was made up of boys who didn't have sisters. "Any of you got a pencil and paper with you? I'll draw you one." Nobody had paper, so I motioned for the others to sit still and ran back into the building and got a couple of sheets and a pencil from my desk, hurried back, and kneeled before Willie as if before God himself, panting, eager to see what he would deliver.

With a yellow pencil he sketched a pussy on a piece of blue-lined paper, the lips as meticulously detailed as anything you might expect in a young Leonardo. When he had finished garnishing the drawing with a vee of curly hair, he tapped the center, where he had so shaded the depths that nothing stood out clearly. "I drawed it spread open. The goodies are in there. Your peter goes right in there."

"What's the hair for?" I asked. I knew women didn't usually have hair on their legs and chests. I had seen *that* much of women.

Willie shook his head. "Ain't got no idea about that. But it's there, after they get to be teenagers."

"You've *seen* one then?" another kid asked him.

"Well, hell yes. My momma's, my sister's, my aunt's. I sneaked and seen'm, but I seen'm. And I done fucked two of my cousins plenty of times."

That news stopped my heart. I wanted to know about it, what it was like, but that was a lesson for another day. Today it was pussy.

"They ain't all that uncommon, you know," Willie said. "Ever teacher walking around this school has got one."

"Except Coach Ellis," someone said. Ellis was a man.

"And all the girls got'm too," Willie said, "but they ain't got hair yet. It's just a tight little ol' slit. Looks like a big butterbean on edge."

"I still don't think I have it straight in my mind." I was really confused by the butterbean business.

"OK, here's what you do. . . ." He looked straight at me. "One of these days I'll take you off somewhere to where you can see one in person—might get one of my cousins to let you fuck her—but for the time being, you take one of your daddy's big ol' boot socks and slide a regular sock down inside of it, past the top of the boot sock. Then roll the top of the boot sock back so that you got a big set of lips, but don't roll the top of the inside sock. It'll look like a set of little thin lips inside the big rolled ones. You'll get a pretty good idea there."

"You might try to get a little bit of it too," one of the other boys put in, snickering, "if you can get it to hold still for you."

"That's funny as the cancer or sugar di-beeteez," I told him.

That afternoon when I got home, while Daddy was still at work and Mother was busy out in the garden and my brother was somewhere playing, I tried it with one of my father's boot socks and one that he wore to church. I tried my very best, and the contraption I wrought might have looked vaguely like a pussy to my untrained eye, but I will tell you quite assertively that I was not the least bit tempted to try it out. Maybe it was the idea that my father's foot had been in there.

I came close to seeing a picture of a naked woman once on a cigarette lighter that one of the boys in the neighborhood had, but that didn't work out either. It was like God had decided that he just wasn't going to let me in on the secret, that he was going to keep toying with me, making me wonder, right on up until I had all my molars and was shaving. While most kids, if they worried about death at all, fretted about how they were going to die and which place they would go to when it happened, I focused on one chilling fact: that I might die before I ever discovered what a girl looked like with her clothes off.

But back to the lighter. . . . There are those memories that linger longer than others, sharper and deeper, like maybe they are sacred and assigned a significance that we might not understand but never question.

We stood that morning at the edge of a creek that ran through a neighbor's pasture, the sun behind the three of us throwing our shadows halfway across the water. My shadow was in the middle, the shortest one, and I remember noting that moving water had absolutely no effect on our shadows, and our shadows no effect on it—the creek just ran right through them. It was hot already, and birds were trilling away in the trees and bushes about us.

"Go ahead," the boy on my left said across me to the boy on my right, the one we called Goober. (I have changed his name to protect him from any shame he might experience from all this.) "Show me how you gon' get fish without a pole."

"How can you do it?" I looked first at Goober, then at the other boy.

Goober said nothing. He just shoved a hand down into his jeans pocket and brought out a cherry bomb.

"This here's how."

He leaned over and scooped up half a crawdad chimney of blue-gray clay, worked it in his hands a minute, then formed it around the red ball, leaving the stem sticking out. From the same pocket he removed a flat silver cigarette lighter that had a woman in some sort of red outfit painted on the side.

"Can I see the lighter?" I asked him.

"You mean the woman." He shook his head. "You ain't old enough. I'll let you look at her another time. Besides this ain't about women. It's about gettin' fish without a pole. Watch."

He flicked open the cover of the lighter and spun a little wheel that showered sparks onto a string that came up right about where the woman's left hand was cut off from her arm; her hand and head were on the lid, sideways now, but she was still smiling. Goober's hand covered most of her from the neck down. The string caught the sparks and flared, sending up a stream of fire as long as my little finger. This was magic enough. My father had once smoked, but quit, and all he ever used was matches. The lighter had a smell about it, exotic, not like the smell of matches.

Goober stepped toward the creek and held the green stem of the cherry bomb to the steady orange flame that smoked a little at the end, the fuse flared and shot fire in all directions, and he leaned out over the edge of the bank, just above the deep hole we often fished in, and slipped the lump of clay into the water and motioned for us to stand back.

For a couple of seconds there was nothing but a small steady stream of bubbles of blue-white smoke that rose to the surface and sizzled, then something jarred the spongy ground we stood on, *krumph,* just as I saw a flash deep in the hole he'd dropped the clay ball in. The water bulged, and a cloud of smoke broke into the air as if some giant had puffed a cigarette on the bottom of the creek. I stood in disbelief as three small bream spun to the surface and floated there until Goober said to the other boy, "There's your fish. Pick'm up."

It was a magic moment for me: the smell of that lighter, on the side of which a nearly naked woman stood, the explosion that jiggled the ground, the bulge of water and puff of blue-white smoke that seemed to come from hell itself, then fish floating up, stunned.

"How can them thangs burn underwater?" the other boy asked him. He had scooped up the bream and cradled them in his shirt front.

"They just can is how," he said, and he lit another in his hand, held it for what seemed like a long time, and threw it high in the air, where it tumbled, fuse fizzing away, until just as it struck the water it exploded and flung a fine spray upon us. Another he held even longer and threw higher. It exploded way above us against that blue deep morning sky, *ka-boom,* and a big cloud of smoke drifted off down the creek.

"Where'd you get it at?" I asked Goober as we walked up toward the pasture. The other kid had headed home with his fish.

"The lighter? My uncle give it to me. He brought it back from France after the war."

"Can I see it?"

He looked at me. "I told you, it ain't the lighter you want to see. It's the woman, ain't it? You gotta admit it."

"Both," I said.

Goober looked wisely at me. "What'll you give me?" He sniffed. "To see her, I mean."

"Pretty much anything I've got, but I ain't got much."

"If you'll run my *Grit* route Saturday, I'll let you hold it for a full minute."

"You'll have to show me where everybody lives at that gets it, but it's a deal."

We shook on it and he handed me the lighter. I studied the woman with the red bathing suit on—two small red spots where her breasts should be, and something like a short skirt for the bottom part—turning her this way and that in the morning sun. The lighter had a decided warmth to it, maybe from Goober's hand, maybe from the flame that had come from it, maybe from. . . . I lifted the lid and watched her head and left hand pivot away from the rest of her, then come magically back together when I closed it.

"She didn't have no clothes on at all, but my aunt painted that bathing suit, or whatever the hell it is on her, with fingernail polish. She said it was a bathing suit."

"You mean she was *nekkid?*"

"As a jaybird," Goober said.

I rubbed my fingertips over the tiny body. "You *seen* her? Without the fingernail polish?"

"Just once, but it was a quick look my uncle give me before my aunt take'n it away from him and covered up the good places."

I studied the woman. "Can we take it off?"

"I thought about that, but what if *she* come off with it? She's painted on too, you know."

"If we was real careful, we might could, with the tip of a knife. I think we ought to try."

"Not if there's a chance she'd scrape off too. Might mess her up. We ain't going to do it."

"I mean just—"

"No. We ain't going to do it. It's *my* woman and *my* goddamn lighter. Now give'm both back."

I handed him the lighter, which still seemed very warm in my hand, like it was alive.

I ran Goober's *Grit* route that Saturday morning, the way I promised. It was a long, hard bicycle ride over gravel, and two dogs almost nailed me, but I made it. For days I thought of fire burning under water, that muffled explosion deep in the creek, and nightly pondered the lady from France on the side of the silver lighter, long blond hair swirled about her lovely face, those long slender legs, wondered what she looked like before Goober's aunt took the polish to her.

On and on it went over the next couple of years, a little bit here and there, but the picture I got loomed more like a Picasso puzzle than a Wyeth, with pieces scattered all about, not fitting together properly, not making any sense. When I had my self-communion, I imagined nothing much at all down there on the girls or women I fancied myself with, just some magic place that took me in and allowed me to do what needed to be done to bring the good feeling on.

Eventually my childhood ran out on me, as they are apt to do, and I made empirical discoveries that explained, at least in part, the many mysteries of the human female body. One day I abandoned my beautiful women in the hay of that barn and never went back for them. I'm certain that my grandfather found them, long after I left them to languish in the dark and fragrant hay, and I am equally certain that he knew how they got there.

So, whether or not it was normal, my mind was preoccupied with sex a good bit of the time when I was growing up. I entertained myself as often as I felt the urge, and the urge was often, and I experimented, as boys will do, with a broad range of substitutes for a reality I would not know for a very long time. Sun-warmed watermelons, large cucumbers, squash—all were fair game, and I saw no harm in using them. No one ever mentioned that a boy might go to hell for pressing vegetables and fruits into such service—nothing in the Bible about it, or I would have heard—and not one of them ever objected.

James Dickey wrote in "The Sheep Child" that "farm boys wild to couple / with anything . . . will keep themselves off / Animals by legends of their own." This was not precisely so out there on Sand Road. I knew boys who ventured into the realm of the four-footed in pursuit of that surrogate pleasure, though I struck out in that direction only once. One moonless September night I accompanied two friends into a pasture not far from the house, where we intended to share our passion with a cow named Blackie, but she was not at all accommodating. The boy first up to bat, teetering on a stump, was soon baptized in the knowledge Yeats so wisely advanced in "Crazy Jane Talks with the Bishop": "Love has pitched his mansion in / The place of excrement." He spent a long while trying to get his T-shirt, jeans, and shorts scrubbed clean in the Cold Hole. What I witnessed that night was a truth as profound as anything I ever carried away from church: that there were easier and safer ways to serve the devil between my thighs.

Girls were a world removed from me. I studied them and worshipped them at distance, but I just didn't know a damned thing about them. I would study them intently in class sometimes, when I was of course supposed to be paying attention to whatever lesson was at hand, but there was just so much I could really see—the rest I had to guess at.

After starting to school, I was infatuated with one girl or another every day of my life, beginning with a girl named Kay Cole, whom I was in first grade with in Millport. I'd swing alongside her at recess singing "You Are My Sunshine" just as loud as my little boy's voice could manage. I never so much as touched her hand. I don't remember who succeeded Kay, after we moved to Mississippi a year after that, but it was probably June Boyd, and then Vickie Waltman, for whom I carried a torch most of my public-school life, though she never knew it. I worshipped her in silence and at great distance. I'd have to list Vivian Loftis and LaWanda Moody and Sally Scales too, and a host of others—all distant stars in my galaxy, bright but cold and very far away. All of them played through my mind as I inched my way to adulthood.

And closer home, there was Marie, the goddess of the Cold Hole.

As streams go, it wasn't much of one then, and it's even less now. But you know how things are for a kid, whose world really doesn't stretch much more than horizon to horizon, even when he realizes that ten miles to the east there's another state, Alabama, where people can buy whiskey and beer, and that somewhere far off there are oceans and mountains. He lives with what he knows. As a boy I knew a few square miles of Luxapalila flood plain, Millport, the church, and school, and for a long time that was the *only* world I knew.

A mile or so north of the house, there was a spring-fed creek that ran as clear as a Colorado trout stream. Most of its water came straight up out of the ground, gushed thirty yards or so, then broke out into a deep, long, wide gravel-bottomed hole that someone, years before I learned about it, dug out and dammed the lower end of. It was called the Cold Hole, the finest swimming place that we knew anything about. The word was that Doc and Pop Byers built the dam, but I cannot confirm that. I do know that Jimmy Densmore and I helped patch it up sometimes after heavy rains gouged it out, so if it had a plaque on it somewhere, I'd insist that our names be listed as the maintenance crew.

In its day—and I say that because it has long since fallen to ruin—the Cold Hole was the place to be in summer. The water was probably somewhere around seventy degrees, judging from what I know of swimming-pool temperatures now, and it would take your breath away when you jumped into it. The gravel dam backed the water up a few feet above its natural level so that at the deepest point a tall man could stand on the bottom and be completely under.

We would usually just jump off the high clay bank on the north side, which was worn as smooth as stone by generations of boys, and from time to time someone would anchor a board for diving. Mostly we just lounged in the Cold Hole, laughing at that blistering Mississippi sun above us, swam a little, and horsed around the way boys will do.

And then there were the special times that we just sat on the bank and watched Marie Byers when she came to swim. Marie, Pop's sister, felt like she had a claim on the Cold Hole, and the Byers lived closest to it, so she'd just show up whenever she wanted to, and when she did, we stopped our foolishness and retreated and watched her. She was the only live girl I had ever seen in a bathing suit, so I was happy to just sit there and study her marvelous female form. Densmore had a sister, but I didn't, so, as I said, there were lots of things about girls that I didn't know and needed to learn. Jimmy told me a few things about her, but he was pretty vague. Marie was in one of the upper grades in high school, and we weren't even in junior high at the time, so she had an entirely different shape from the girls we went to school with—you know what I mean.

We'd be down at the Cold Hole swimming and jumping off the bank, yelling, just generally horsing around, and somebody would whisper, "Lord, here she comes," and we'd freeze in whatever position we were in, collect ourselves, slither out like what she probably judged to be primordial life forms, and turn the pool over to her. Then the goddess descended. Since there was always a chance Marie would show up, we never skinny-dipped in the Cold Hole except at night.

Marie wouldn't even look at us. With a classy little flourish, she'd remove her towel from her shoulders, lay it on a nearby cypress stump, walk down to the edge of the dam, and dangle a foot in, jerk it back, then just stand there for a few minutes studying the water, waiting for the pool to purge itself of our filth, flush it on downstream. No telling how boys might foul a swimming hole.

She always wore a black swimsuit, one piece, and her skin was astonishingly white against it. Her hair, very long and straight like an Indian's, was almost as dark as the suit, and it reminded me of that kind of clean-looking sheen a horse's tail has in the sun. Yep, in my mind she was a goddess.

Then she'd boldly wade out into that cold water—past her ankles, past her knees, then up to her waist. I remember marveling at how the water would make her legs look fat and short, like something made of wax, melted down and compacted below the waist. Finally she'd launch out into the pool and her body would resume its fine shape, and she'd swim back and forth a few times, using the smoothest, most marvelous strokes I'd ever seen. I wasn't far beyond the dog-paddling stage, so it didn't take much to impress me.

When she'd finished her swim, Marie would wade out, dry herself off with the towel, then walk back up the wooded path toward home, never once having looked at us. Somebody gave the signal, and I would come out of my trance, start breathing again, and leap into that water, which seemed warmer than it had been before she descended.

One winter day several years ago my wife and I walked down to where the Cold Hole had been, but I wish we hadn't, with the dam long since washed away, the place choked with leaves and limbs, the stream the color of tea. Standing there where once Marie Byers had dangled her foot into that crystal water, I felt the same sadness I have felt at Pompeii and other ruins where only desolation abounds, the lifeblood drained away, all the gods and goddesses gone.

And, oh, there was Judy Morris.

When I was growing up, kudzu was in such demand for erosion control in Mississippi that some farmers actually grew the stuff for planting. Three miles or so down Sand Road a Mr. Morris had a kudzu farm with acres and acres of sprigs, which looked like sweet potato slips. He would grow them to a certain point, then harvest the runners for distribution to the state highway department, who would plant them along roadbeds. Within a matter of months the vines would take a good foothold, and nothing short of a bulldozer could loosen the soil they had seized. I mean, that stuff would completely swallow a barn and smother full-grown trees. It spread across the South like a green gospel.

Weekends I would hang out down at Mr. Morris's farm a lot, mostly because he had a blond-haired daughter named Judy, who was drop-dead movie-star gorgeous and smart to boot and popular; she was an officer in more school organizations than you could shake a kudzu vine at. I don't even know for sure that he was her father, but someone told me so, and that was good enough for me. Whether Judy ever went down there, I don't know, but I had it firmly fixed in my mind that someday she might, and I hoped to be there if she did.

If she *had* shown up, I cannot imagine what I expected to happen when she got there. Would she get naked and go swimming in the Luxapalila, which ran alongside the place, or maybe strip down to a bathing suit and sunbathe out by the kudzu? I just didn't know, but I wanted to be there when it happened. Just thinking about her—as I lounged about in the kudzu that had escaped Mr. Morris's careful rows and lay like a coarse green shawl on the riverbank—made my heart do that weird climb into my throat.

Some days I'd play on Mr. Morris's Ford tractor, an old 9N, which he kept parked down by the river, nose pointed away from it. I'd pretend to drive it, go through the gears, make tractor sounds with my tongue and lips. One day I discovered that with the tractor in gear I could push the starter (a little button that you pressed with your foot—it looked like one of the old dimmer switches cars and trucks used to have on the floorboard) and make it inch forward up out of the wild kudzu and onto the gravel road that ran along the river, then back it up again, and this I did, over and over. It was slow, but *I was driving a tractor!* When the battery started draining down, I'd let it rest until my next trip.

But one day something strange happened that kept me off his tractor and away from his kudzu farm for good. I'd inched the machine into the road and was backing up when the starter hung, and that tractor kept inching toward the bluff over the river, *rhu-rhu-rhu-rhu.* In desperation I kicked it out of gear with my foot and hit the brakes and stopped it just shy of the river. I held the brakes while the starter kept going until the battery ran down, then I put it in gear and left it precariously perched in a netting of vines. I don't know how much purchase those tires had on the bank, but I'm sure that if the kudzu had not been there, the tractor would have disappeared into that murky water.

After that I came a little bit to my senses about the possibility of Judy showing up and the chances I was taking waiting for her. If Mr. Morris caught me down there, it would explain a lot about run-down tractor batteries and that old 9N left perched at the edge of the river.

I suspect that Judy Morris never knew I existed, but I had these wild notions that she'd show up down there at the kudzu farm one day and maybe *talk* to me awhile at least, even if she didn't go skinny dipping or sunbathe by the kudzu. If she'd said to me, "Hey, boy, I'll let you kiss me if you'll eat six row feet of kudzu," I'd have asked, "What'll you let me do if I eat a *whole* row?"

Well, the last time I was down at the kudzu farm, it was obvious that Mr. Morris's strict mastery of the vines had long since disappeared. They had taken the whole place—a two to four foot thick carpet of steamy green stretched from field edge to field edge, mounding over trees, and ended only where it drooped off into the Luxapalila.

I didn't linger long, but I did stand there about where that old tractor used to be parked and wonder whether Judy ever showed up, ever graced the place with her gorgeous presence, and I smiled as I remembered all those days of waiting for her when she didn't even know I was there, back when the kudzu was fairly tame, my imagination the only thing out of control.

I constantly fell in love with teachers, such as Betty Sutton, who taught science, and once I found myself totally taken with a—uh, yep, you're about to read me right—a *librarian.*

Unmarried, she was a slender, angular woman, like something stamped out of sheet metal—all corners and edges, it seemed to me. She carried herself the way some PE teachers do, arms curled like parentheses, and when she walked, her stride was manly. She seemed not to mind that in that place of graveyard quiet her shoes sounded like thunder, like a stormy sky warning you that lightning is near. We could hear her from one end of the library to the other, down one aisle, up another—clump, clump, clump—and when the thunder neared, we cringed and held our breath.

Her unadorned hands were always red and raw, something from the world of work and cold or maybe from fire or the agitation of wringing, and when I read Shakespeare's poetic description of Greasy Joan keeling the pot, though it was Marian's nose that was red and raw, I imagined Miss Bennett (name changed to protect her from the curious) snatching from Joan the spoon or paddle, or whatever one keels a pot with, and swirling like the Macbeth witches, boiling children until they were tender enough to chew. On her hands she wore a poignant lotion that smelled of turpentine and shone like mayonnaise—but they always looked like they had been in fire or in cold. She touched me only once that I can remember, her hand swooping down swift as lightning onto my arm, and her fingers, neither hot nor cold, were hard as talons.

She was a woman who seldom smiled, and when she did, it was a sidelong toothy grin that might well have been a snarl. I thought of jacks and grinnel, fish whose teeth could shear a perch in two with one smooth strike. Her eyes were always without mirth or softness, and they shot around the library, the hunting eyes of a hawk, looking for something to descend upon. They were a frightening cold blue, frigid pools in their snowcaps, and when they fell upon us we cringed. Her aquiline nose and her hair, close-cropped and swept back, made her look even more like a predatory bird.

But one spring day something happened that created in me a fascination for her that from that day on would not let me rest. It was a study period, and I was trying hard to concentrate on whatever was at hand—decidedly not schoolwork—when she clumped past the table I was seated at and reached to retrieve a book from a shelf. As she did, her right foot tilted forward out of her shoe, revealing along the bottom edge, very near the heel, a tattoo, small and oval and blue, and inside it the name *John*. Before I could get anyone else's attention, the foot had settled back in the shoe, and the tattoo disappeared.

But I know what I saw that day, and it burned in my mind for weeks; every time I saw her, I glanced at her foot to see if she might again reveal her dark secret, but she never did.

Sometimes at night, before sleep, as the sounds of crickets and frogs blended with the squawking belt of the Sears window fan in the kitchen and the spring air drifted across my bed, I would have strange feelings as I imagined Miss Bennett's white ankles and lovely calves, and I wondered who John was and where he might be and what she was like back there long ago when she thought enough of him to have his name branded on her, what wild and wicked music she danced to, how she wore her hair. As I stared at the shadowy ceiling and thought of her, Miss Bennett seemed like a different woman, her touch soft, her hair long and lovely, her eyes a liquid fire that warmed me and lulled me off to sleep

And then there was the tight-rope walker. . . .

It was perhaps my twelfth year under the light of the meat-eating sun, as the poet Dylan Thomas so poignantly put it, that she came into my life, and she has never really left.

Oh, Lord, how I do remember her skinny little body so tightly bound by the silken silver outfit she wore that every bone stood out, ribs and pelvis and vertebrae and, high on her back, the nubs of her sprouting wings. She walked within touching distance, as untouchable as the angels, her eyes fixed straight ahead, and all I could do was stare and try to quell my hammering heart. That blond hair and pale, celestial face, those thin arms and legs, every line of muscle and bone, chest flat as a boy's, and about her the faint scent of spices. She didn't look at me. She didn't have to. It was enough that I was permitted by the gods to see her.

Septembers the fair came to our little Mississippi town, as surely as football seasons, welcomed with an almost frenzy by the kids who were still too young to be swept up in the sweat and agony of the gridiron. And even more by the country kids who rode their bikes down dusty back roads to the glitter and the glare, then back out under the eerie light of the moon or simple stars, penniless, with the sticky sweet of cotton candy still clinging to their faces and the throb of the midway dancing from ear to ear.

It was September, and I was there. Midafternoon, sweaty from the long ride, I leaned my old bicycle against an oak at the edge of the fairgrounds and secured it with a double-knotted rope (more than adequate in those days to keep it safe, as if anyone else would have had it) and booth by booth frittered away the hours and precious coins: flung softballs at concrete bottles squatting like stone soldiers, threw darts at balloons that dodged and weaved with every ribbon of air, and slammed around the oval bumper-car court. I kept deep down in my pocket a quarter, sacred and reserved for the Big Top, and waited for the night to come.

Finally the afternoon waned, the sun relented, and I joined a chattering band, who for all their fervor might well be going that very night to some great, stirring revival meeting where angels would be witnessed and miracles and maybe even the Holy Face Itself. For what we were going to see could not be seen elsewhere in our little lives: the magic of the Big Top, as fascinating for me as what went on under the revival tents, where the lame threw down their crutches and the blind were blessed with dazzling sight. On impulse—I cannot tell you why, for most of my life in those days was mystery and whim—I broke from the ranks and slipped around behind the tent, in my pocket my only prize for the day, a fuzzy rabbit foot strung on a chain. I rubbed it for luck as I stood at a back flap, hoping no one would discover me and chase me off. And luck it brought me: this shining girl, the tight-rope walker.

With a man who might have been her father—a burly chap with hairy shoulders and back and arms—she descended from a trailer, a burnished aluminum loaf that squatted behind the tent, and followed him past me and through the flap, disappearing into the shadows from which muffled music came. I stood a long time looking at the slit through which she had entered, until applause and children's shrieks brought me back and I hurried around to the front, paid my quarter, and went inside.

What a delight were the elephant and two tigers and one lone, crippled lion, who in another tent, under evangelist Thelma Bentley's curing hands, would have sprung whole again, king of the jungle, proud and nimble. They gamboled about the single sawdust ring, spurred by two men with whips, until our hands stung with battering applause and our throats ached with yelling.

And then from behind a curtain came the man and little girl, mounting the pole as if gravity no longer mattered. One smooth step off the circular platform, four or five silken strides, and he was across to the other platform, followed by the girl, a nimbus of motion. Back and forth they went through the insect-stirred air, back and forth, until my uplifted head reeled with her silver sheen. My eyes never left her. For a finale she threw herself into his arms, whereupon he swept her to the side and up onto his shoulders, and she stood balanced, arms outstretched, as he crossed the wire again.

On my ride home that night I could feel the first lilt of fall coming on even before I had dipped into the night-cool hollow of the low-water crossing on McBee Creek. But it was not fall I was thinking of, not the grinding of my wheels through heavy gravel or their whir through foot-deep water, not the notion that I still had two hard miles to go to home and bed. On that moon-bathed, lonesome road I thought of nothing but the silver girl suspended against a canvas sky, defying all that we fear.

Sometimes I think of her now, when an uncertain mood settles on me, like the feeling you get in early spring when the earth rekindles—tongueless and indefinable—and the music of that September night comes back and echoes in my head. There is an ache, an emptiness, that nothing can really satisfy or fill, and I think I prefer it that way. I used to wonder what might have happened to her, where she is now, what perilous balance she keeps, whether time has been gentle or cruel. But I am content to remember my silver tight-rope walker as she was one September night long ago—when to her gravity was a minor force and mattered no more than death—a shining angel suspended above the sawdust earth and our upturned faces that saw in the insect-stirred air nothing but light, light, light.

Later on, as I gradually grew into an awareness of the fact that girls might, after all, be something of this earth and thereby accessible, I began entertaining the notion of maybe actually *being* with one. And I finally kissed a girl.

It was a long time ago, and we were innocent and naive, with little to worry us beyond the notion that Russian rockets might someday rain down on Columbus Air Force Base, and, according to our parents, we would all evaporate in an instant or suffer slow, agonizing deaths from radiation poisoning. Most of us kids didn't know much about the nature of the threat, though, and didn't care—we knew we were immortal and would survive. Such is the irrepressible nature of youth.

Jamie Dagress was a freshman and I a sophomore at Lee High School when we finally got together one late spring evening over at Julia Baker's house, probably three or four miles away by bike. Jimmy Densmore was going to see Julia, and Jamie was spending the night with her. I got invited along so that Jamie wouldn't feel left out while the other two were doing whatever they were going to be doing. This was fine with me, because Jamie was pretty and smart, and she was a *girl.*

My mind was all aswirl as we pedaled along in the twilight toward my first date. We both had to ride bicycles if we wanted to go anywhere too far to walk. I didn't really know what a guy did on a date when he didn't have a car to go parking in. You couldn't say to a girl, "Hey, baby, let's go riding," knowing that should she agree to go with you, and you were lucky enough for things to begin to warm up, you couldn't just invite her to move to the backseat with you. Well, I guess you could. . . .

I don't remember what Julia and Jimmy did that evening, but Jamie and I went walking, and in time we settled on the dark steps of Fairview

Elementary School. We talked awhile—about what, I have no idea—and in time our bodies just naturally gravitated toward each other, and I put my arm around her waist, a pretty daring thing for a guy with absolutely no experience in the field. Then, my confidence growing, I tried to touch my face to hers, but Jamie wore these really wild glasses with some sort of flared hinge that gouged the corner of my right eye every time I got close. I finally asked her whether she would take them off. And she did. It was the first time a girl had ever taken anything off for me, so I was proud and emboldened.

I can't say at what point I summoned the nerve to ask her, but after a long spell I whispered, "Would you like to kiss?" When she said she guessed so, my breathing stopped, and I don't believe it started again until we were finished. We turned to face each other, and our lips met, tight and intent. She probably didn't have much more experience than I did, if any, so it was like touching my lips to the muzzle of a Coca-Cola bottle, a firm little ring and nothing more, just warmer. For what seemed like an eternity we were pressed together like that, and everything in my small universe stopped dead still except for my thrashing heart, which eventually I forced back down into its bony cage. I don't know whether a boy can hold his breath for two minutes or not, but under those conditions he might.

That was it for the school steps, since we'd really made a great leap there. Nervous and silent, we walked back to Julia's house, holding hands. Jimmy and Julia were off somewhere when we got back, so we decided to sit on the porch and talk, but I guess too great a gulf had been crossed and we were trying hard to fathom it. We just sat there in silence leaning back against the front of the house and listening to the crickets and tree frogs razzing until on over in the night sometime Jamie leaned her head against my shoulder and fell sound asleep.

This sort of thing could trounce the egos of most guys, but I viewed it as an opportunity to experiment, and off I went. With her fast asleep beside me, I eased her head back against the wall, rotated my body, and kissed her. I describe a similar scene in my novel *Castle in the Gloom:* "She did not respond, so I went down again, this time relaxing my lips like a mouth-breather and wallowing them against hers, the way I had seen people do it in movies. As her lips slackened against mine, I kept thinking that it was like kissing plastic fishing worms that smelled faintly of grape Kool-Aid, all loose and slick and rolling around and utterly lifeless." I did nothing more wicked that night, but I rode home with the exhilaration of triumph pounding in my head and deep in my chest a sense of shame for taking advantage of an unconscious girl who would never know what I had done.

Later on I would occasionally go over to her house on the south side of Columbus. We'd smooch some, but that was as far as I got. On the way over there one blistering summer day, a ride of seven or eight miles, I stopped by a store near her house and bought two Eskimo Pies. I knew nothing of courting amenities, but I reasoned that if I were a girl and had someone coming to visit me on such a hot summer day, I'd want an Eskimo Pie, not some goofy flowers. But my chain came off only a block away from the store and there I was, needing both hands to put the chain back on and those Eskimo Pies going soft fast, so I did the only thing I could think of: I ate them both, hers first, so that I would enjoy it more. I didn't have enough money to go back for another, so I chewed a piece of spearmint to cover up the smell of chocolate and ice cream and rode on to her house. (Several years ago I wrote a column piece about it and apologized to Jamie for eating her Eskimo Pie. It was awfully good, and I was wicked for eating it, but what else was there to do? Her mother read the piece and sent it to her, and we had a reunion at my wife's parents' house on the Mississippi coast. We did not kiss.)

And then there was Alice (named changed to protect her honor).

The first time I saw her, one early September morning, she was getting on the school bus in front of the house her family had moved into on Highway 50, a little over a mile from mine by road, a bit less across Jim Bob Field's and Boyd Shelton's pastures. For days I studied the back of her head on the way to school. Then I fell for her, hard: the bright blond hair that stopped at her shoulders (so unlike the girls who went to the Assembly of God church I attended, who wore theirs almost to the backs of their knees), bird-egg-blue eyes that burned at twenty yards, and skin so smooth and white it was almost translucent. Sure, she was skinny, but so was every kid I knew out our way. The Nation of Obesity was decades and millions of tons of refined foods in the future.

Alice was a year or two younger than I was, and I wanted more than anything else in the world to date her. I wasn't sure what one did on a date, since I'd never been on an official one. I wanted to see her up close, talk to her, hold her hand, maybe—well, I guess what I *really* wanted to do was *kiss* her. I mean, I had already kissed a girl, so I knew what to expect. I just didn't have any notion how to go about getting to that stage with Alice.

But Nature works in mysterious ways her wonders to perform. We note it in male lizards, who puff their throats to a cherry red before females, and in peacocks, who flare their gaudy tails. Roosters strut and preen, bucks bang each other head-on until the victor wins the doe, and male dogs will kill themselves battling for the favors of a female. (I saw this once. Three dogs were fighting over a little thing they'd hounded for hours, and the smallest of the lot, who kept getting tossed out of the fray, just slipped off with the girl while the two big ones fought away in a whirlwind of dust and fur. I think Nature had not intended it to work that way, but the little male seemed content enough with the contract, and the female didn't care who took care of her needs.) We may not understand the reasoning behind Nature's message, but when we don't have other options, we do as she says.

So I let Nature take over. After school and on weekends I started climbing into one of the pines across the highway from Alice's house and whooping—a sort of Tarzan thing, profoundly simian, but recall that I was simply following Nature. I swung from limb to limb, bellowing and grunting and shrieking. I suppose I banged my bony chest, though through the mist I cannot see or hear it. For days I did this. The wonder is that someone didn't shoot me or have me locked up.

If this seems awfully immature for someone my age, I plead ignorance. My parents had not taught me a single damned thing about how to get a girl, and we didn't have a television set, where I might have gotten some pointers. The boys I grew up around were as clueless as I was, and the city kids lived in their own world of cars and televisions and bright lights and didn't have the time or patience to teach me such fundamental lessons. I was on my own.

One afternoon, late, Alice walked across the highway and stared up into the tree where I crouched, my bare feet draped across a limb, steady as an ape.

"Hi-dy," I said to her uplifted face, making conversation. "You the new girl?"

She squinted at me, said "Yes," then pointed across the highway. "I live there." Like I didn't know that. But I'm pretty certain she didn't know who I was, because I got on the bus before she did and always sat in the very back, where bouncing was best on the Sand Road loop.

She moved farther beneath the tree and shaded her eyes. "What are you doing up that tree, boy?"

"Nothing," I told her and swung down, Tarzan fashion, fumbled on the lowest limb, and made a five-point landing, butt and heels and palms of the hand, at her feet. After righting myself and brushing off pine needles, I fell in behind her as she walked back across to her yard. She didn't invite me to follow her but didn't say I couldn't, so I decided I'd see just how far this thing would go. I kept my eyes on her hair.

When we passed the corner of the house, a curtain cracked and I saw one of her momma's eyes studying the primate that had been aloose in the trees across the road and now her daughter was bringing into the yard, without so much as a rope around its neck. Out back Alice offered me a seat in a lawn chair and said she'd go in and get a couple of co-colas, that I was probably thirsty after all that hollering. I was.

We sat awhile and talked, about school and the neighborhood. I kept looking around to make certain her father wasn't home. When the Cokes were finished, I left.

And that was that. I had seen her up close, and I liked what I saw. A few days later I started crossing the pastures to her house as often as she'd let me, and we'd sit in lawn chairs side by side in the dark backyard, just talking and looking up at the stars.

Finally, after what seemed to me a much longer warming up period than was necessary, maybe a couple of weeks, she let me hold her hand and one special night we sat in a swing together and she permitted me to kiss her. I could smell a faint trace of soap on her skin, and when I held her close to me, I could smell her hair. It was like nothing I'd ever breathed. There was no fragrance of shampoo or anything like that, just her hair. *Angel hair,* I kept thinking. But not like that stuff we threw on Christmas trees. I mean, *real* angel hair that smelled nice. I could have kept my face there forever.

Alas, it was a short affair with little growth potential, as is sometimes said of investments. I had woefully limited resources, and any place we went we would have to go on my bicycle or walk, and when we got there, I had no money to spend. That far out of town the only thing within easy reach was Dowdle's Store to the west and McBee Church to the east, neither of which Alice seemed terribly interested in. After a few weeks, she must have gotten the idea that I didn't care whether we went anywhere or not, as long as she'd let me hold and kiss her and bury my face in her hair. I guess girls weary of such attention.

One night in the swing in her backyard I was in the process of attempting an escalation when she moved my hand from where I had allowed it to fall casually on her knee and announced that her parents thought she had started seeing too much of me and would prefer that we, as they say, *cool it.* In short, the monkey ought to go back to whatever jungle it had come from.

A rejected and dejected lad, that night I crossed the pastures under a sky ablaze with stars, the smell of Alice's hair lingering in my head like the faint glow of a heaven I could never know. I felt like a traveler lost in space. The year was on a fast wane, air pulsed a little from the north, chill and damp. In another few weeks the trees, already changing, would start to thin. Far across the fences and fields behind me I could see the lights of her house twinkling, and ahead in the dark a lone bulb shone above our back-porch door.

I never went back to my tree.

After Alice concluded that our relationship was not bearing precisely the sort of fruit she thought it should—though I would have done anything she asked to keep myself in her favor—I didn't go over to her house again or call her or in any way attempt to make contact, not even on the school bus, which is where many a romance in those days out there where I lived began and flourished and sometimes died, right there on the Sand Road loop. (One boy was caught alongside a girl with his pants down at his knees, and when the bus driver was advised that something evil was going on at the back of the bus, he stopped and stalked up the aisle, only to be advised by the two of them that they were looking for ticks. He nodded and went back and finished his route. Only in Mississippi. . . .) For a year or so I gave her little thought. That is a lie: I thought about her a lot, but I couldn't summon the courage to act.

Now it came to pass that during my junior year in high school my father, who'd been having some sort of circulation problem, which he just necessarily attributed to his stretch of service with the army in Germany in the months immediately following WWII, where the winters were appreciably colder than what he was accustomed to in Alabama, accepted the government's invitation to spend a couple of weeks in Memphis at a veterans' hospital. Since it wouldn't cost him anything, he decided to let the doctors give him a good going over and come on back home cured as a Christmas ham.

The big problem was how Mother would get to her job at Bank's Hardware in downtown Columbus and buy groceries and how the family would get to church. The latter was his greatest concern, since if we skipped a Wednesday night or Sunday morning or evening service, the devil, waiting right down there in the Luxapalila bottoms, would come slinking like a gypsy in the dark and snatch us up, sling us across his shoulder, and tote us straight to hell. Those were the days before you got to go in luxury in a handbasket or a Walmart shopping cart.

Daddy had a car, a '53 Chevrolet sedan, yellow with green trim. But I had never sat behind the wheel of it without him at my right elbow, his voice bellowing: "Jesus Christ, boy, easy on that clutch!" "You can climb any hill in Alabama or Mississippi in second." "Let off the gas!!!!" "Slow down in them curves, son!" "My God, boy, you will *never* learn to drive!"

I mean, I had already taken driver's ed under Coach Carr at Lee High, and I had a driver's license, which was about as much use to me as a bank passbook, since I didn't have a car *or* any money. When I went anywhere too far to walk, I rode my bike or hitchhiked. I damn well knew how to drive a car, but never to suit Daddy. He'd take me over into the hills of Alabama south of Millport and let me drive where it wasn't likely we'd encounter much traffic—we were lucky enough to encounter a *road*—and all the while he hunkered over me, ready to grab the wheel or slide his foot across and hit the brake. I might as well have been sitting in his lap like a five year old.

But when he had to go to Memphis, he couldn't leave Mother without a ride, and his pride wouldn't let him ask someone else to drive her, even with Uncle Dwight living two doors down. He and Mother discussed the possibility of calling a taxi, but they figured it would cost an eye and ear (or arm and leg, if you want to use a cliché) for one to come that far out into the country, if one would come at all.

Well, the evening before he was to head up to Memphis, he called me onto the back steps and motioned for me to sit down beside him. He had a worried look, so I had no idea what was coming. It was the face he took on when he and Mother talked about so and so coming down with *the cancer.*

"Now, son," he said, after he'd cleared his throat twice.

"Yessir?"

"You know where I got to go tomar, and you know I'm gon' be up there several days." He cleared his throat again. "Now, you are pretty much full-growed and you know how to drive and you got a license, so. . . ."

My heart had already started fluttering and rising, kinda like a big fat hen trying to fly, feathers and dust everywhere and all kinds of commotion.

"So I am gon' catch a bus to Memphis in the morning and leave the car here for you to drive your momma around." He held out his key chain to me.

You remember that big hen I was talking about? Well, it rose like a quail. My heart was in my throat, big as your present-day Butterball roaster.

"I'm gon' drive to the bus station, and then you got to drive right back home. I done wrote the miles down, and your momma is gon' write down the miles ever day until I get back. You ain't to take that car nowhere at all without she is in it too. And you are to drive twenty in town and no faster than forty outside town. I'll be able to tell if you hotrod it."

Now, he was talking about a six cylinder that would barely spin in mud, and he was holding me to forty, which was ten miles-per-hour under that perilous maximum of fifty that he allowed himself on the highway. *Hotrod it, hell,* I was thinking. *About like hotrodding our push mower.*

But all I said was, "Yessir."

Then he took me around to the carport and pointed out every single part of the engine that he could name and told me what to look for if it started leaking or making a funny noise or anything. He showed me for the thousandth time how to check the oil and water and tires. I mean, it was like he was showing me the car for the first time and he was going to be gone a decade.

He started inside, then stopped. "That car's gon' be in *your* hands, boy."

So there I was in possession of the family car for at least two weeks, maybe longer, depending on how long it would take the probing doctors at the veterans' hospital in Memphis to discover why my father's toes went numb when he was hunting in low-teens weather and wearing nothing on his feet but regular wool socks and ordinary boots. I thought about suggesting to him why it happened, but I wanted that car to myself more than I wanted to save him the trip to Memphis.

I stood there a long time looking at that old Chevy, imagining what it would be like to drive it without him perched on my shoulder like some kind of nosy guardian angel. I got to thinking about Mother perched on my shoulder instead, and that took some glory out of it. But hey, I was about to solo in Daddy's car!

The following Sunday afternoon, after I had made the ferry run from church to home and Mother had fixed her usual Sabbath spread of fried chicken, with creamed potatoes and gravy and green beans and cornbread, topped off with peach cobbler, an idea came barging into my head like a Russian boar.

"Mother," I said sweetly. I sidled up like a shy dog as she finished the dishes, "the battry on that car is awful low. It would barely crank this morning. I 'spect I ought to take it out on the highway and drive it a little and build a charge on it. If I don't, it might not crank in the morning, and I won't be able to take you to work. Them short trips to town and to church just ain't puttin' much juice in it."

She gave me that look that mothers reserve for children who they figure are likely lying, but they're not totally sure. I can't even really describe it, so I won't try. But you who have seen it know what I'm talking about.

"How many miles?" she asked. "And how long?"

"Well, I figger maybe half a' hour or something like that. Long enough for the generator to pump enough juice into the battry." (They were generators in those days, long before they got college degrees and became alternators. Call them what you will, they juiced up the battry. Yeah, we called them *battries,* mainly because that's the only way we ever heard the word pronounced, and electricity was *juice.*)

"Well, let me change my clothes, and you can take me to Millport, and we'll visit with Momma'nem."

That is precisely what I figured she would propose, so I just told her that I didn't want to overdo it and use up all the gas, since I had never filled the car and wasn't sure how to do it, and I didn't have any money for gas anyway. Daddy had topped it up on the way to the bus station Monday morning, and he told me that it would be enough to last till he got back, meaning that it had better.

It worked, and she backed off. And my plan fell into place.

Around three o'clock the car was idling in Alice's driveway while I eased up onto the porch and rapped lightly on the door. In a few seconds she cracked it a couple of inches, saw who it was, and asked, "What do you want?"

"I thought maybe you'd like to go riding."

She cracked the door a little more and peeped out. "In a *car?*"

Now, this was not really such a dumb question, since the only time she'd ridden with me before, and that was twice, we were on my bicycle.

"Yep." I pointed to the Chevy. "A car. I got it for the afternoon."

Well, I won't begin to try to tell you how fast she switched attitudes on me—I'm talking about completely reversing gears. In a heartbeat she was in that seat beside me. and we were tooling, right at forty, east on Highway 50. Her folks were off visiting with relatives, she said, and she was bad bored, so a car ride just wedged nicely into her Sunday afternoon schedule.

OK, you don't have to guess what I had on my mind. I wanted a place to park, and fast. I knew Mother would be watching the long clock hand drop slowly down to the six and labor back up, so I would have to make my move like a male in the lower animal kingdom, instinctive and swift.

It had rained earlier in the week, damn it, so every decent parking road was boggy, and the very last thing I needed was to have to slog out in search of somebody with a tractor to pull me to solid ground. What I decided, then, was to stay on one of the back gravel roads that led onto the old Marshall Place way up Sand Road. There were few ruts, since the roads were traveled mainly by trucks hauling sand and gravel from the pits way out in what during WWII had been an emergency landing field for the air base, and they jiggled out enough overflow to keep the footing firm.

I drove slowly out into the middle of a vast field of cotton. It was mid-July and hot as a June bride draped with a horse blanket canning green beans